THE
PICNIC
BOOK

THE PICNIC BOOK

Ali Ray

AA

Published by AA Publishing, a trading name of
AA Media Limited, whose registered office is Fanum House, Basing View,
Basingstoke, Hampshire RG21 4EA; registered number 06112600.

First published in 2019
10 9 8 7 6 5 4 3 2 1

A CIP catalogue record for this book is available from the British Library.

ISBN: 978-0-7495-8115-2

Art Director: James Tims
Editor: Clare Ashton
Design concept: Tom Whitlock
Page layout: Tracey Freestone
Colour reprographics: Ian Little

Photography by James Tims

Map on page 14 © Elizabeth Baldin. Created using relief shading from
Mountain High Maps® Copyright © 1993 Digital Wisdom®, Inc

Cover background image © Andrey Kuzmin/Alamy Stock Photos
Vector graphics © Binkski/Alamy Stock Photos

Printed and bound in China by
1010 Printing Group Limited

A05655

CONTENTS

FOOD FOR OUTDOOR ADVENTURES

Nothing says freedom and happiness like eating your food out in the fresh air. A meal served on a picnic rug indicates the rules are off and we're released from the restrictions of table manners and awkward cutlery. A picnic gives diners permission to be carefree.

A simple sandwich scoffed on a bench away from the office at lunchtime serves to nourish the spirit as well as the body, while a lunch-in-your-lap can turn a walker's rest stop into an occasion. The great thing about picnics is that they suit everyone, young or old; whether you want to be active with kids, to sit on a rug with a loved one or decide to organise something fancy for a group of mates on a beach. However grand or modest, a meal outside can create a memory out of any meal.

For me, having a picnic brings together the best things in life: food, friends, family and best of all, being in the fresh air. I enjoy it so much it has become my job.

It started in my twenties when I taught myself to cook. At the time I was living in my campervan with my husband-to-be travelling around Australia. It meant I learned to cook all meals on a small picnic table outside rather than in a kitchen. It was a very relaxing way to prepare a meal – and to eat. Before each meal, we'd stop the van next to a great view, the beach or a woodland. I chopped and cooked while the birds sang overhead. Beautiful, outdoor surroundings became our dining room.

On returning to England, I began to write travel and food articles and recipes for newspapers and magazines. For the past 10 years I have written a monthly food column in a camping magazine with recipes and ideas for where to buy local British produce, what to make with it and where to eat it. It means my family and I travel and camp a lot around Britain, spending a great deal of our time outside, walking, cycling and being at the beach. I've had to create the type of meal that suits this lifestyle – picnics – and many of these recipes are in this book.

This is a cook book for people who love spending time outdoors. It provides recipes for great meals on the move, from simple dishes that you can sling on your back for a day's hike or bike ride to a picnic for a big family gathering in the park. There are recipes for a romantic picnic for two, ideas for creating big outdoor feasts for friends, a power picnic for cyclists and a posh hamper full of goodies for dining on manicured lawns.

Being an avid griller, it would seem odd to me not to include a chapter on barbecuing in a book about eating outside. After all, cooking outside is as much of a joy. I love the way a barbecue draws guests to it like moths to a flame. A chat over the charcoal while the feast is cooking is such a wonderfully chilled out way to prepare a meal. I'm always heartened when I see public barbecuing areas in Britain, as it was a feature of Australian life I enjoyed so much. I've included some of the ones I've found in the picnic spots.

There are menu ideas at the end of each chapter that will inspire you to create a fantastic spread for your picnic. I've covered a wide range of occasions, so you should find the menu to suit you – or mix and match as much as you want. In some cases, I've pulled in recipes from other chapters to give you more options. Whatever your open-air adventure, there's a moveable menu in this book for you.

PICNIC SPOTS

With my job I've travelled all around the globe but, hands down, I still consider Great Britain to be the most beautiful place in the world. We are blessed with such variety in our island nation: the mountains of Wales and Scotland, the dramatic north Cornish coastline, the vast skies of Norfolk, mysterious Somerset wetlands, the quaintness of the Cotswolds, the majesty of the Scottish Highlands, canals, waterfalls, ancient woodlands, lakes, fells, moorland. Lucky us. There is a nook, cranny, view, cove and dell to suit all tastes, moods and gatherings. That's before we even consider the wealth of history and heritage surrounding us: we have access to exquisite formal gardens as well as atmospheric ruins of ancient abbeys and castles.

Throw in the changing seasons and we are treated to an ever-changing set of beautiful backdrops for our feasts.

At the end of each chapter I have included some of my favourite places to spread a picnic rug, as well as those of my travelling friends and colleagues. Some are secret 'seek-them-out' spots, others are well known. Sometimes there are suggestions for the best time of day to visit, usually to watch the sun rise or set, or I've added a little bit of detail about the geology or quirky local history. Many are free to access, others charge a fee or a parking charge, but they are so lovely I consider it well worth it for a day out.

For the children's picnic spots I've picked locations with an extra bit of entertainment nearby, usually in the form of nature's playground: babbling brooks to dip in, trees with rope swings or country parks with playgrounds. They're close to where you park the car to avoid any whinging about walking too far, and most importantly there are loos nearby.

Picnics can be especially romantic occasions, so for these loved-up locations, I've chosen places you could have a supper under the stars among the sand dunes, and even a picnic spot for a proposal (my husband proposed to me at a picnic on a beach at sunset). Sometimes love is as simple as sharing a beautiful view, a great cake and a flask of tea.

I came up with the idea for this book while sitting high up on a cliff, overlooking Mewslade Bay on the Pembrokeshire coastal path. Half way along the walk, my husband and I stopped to eat the lunch in our backpack. There was a large horizontal slab of stone jutting out above the path – so we sat at either side of it like it was our own personal grand dining table with one of the most beautiful views in the world. Picnic perfection. I still remember it 10 years on. Those are the kind of moments I hope to inspire you with through this book.

KIT AND CABOODLE

Another key factor in picnic success is making sure you have the right kit. I am not referring to a need for multiple designer picnic rugs and a dinner service. Good picnic kits involve the 'don't forgets' such as the chopping board and knife, the bin bags and kitchen towels.

First and foremost, you need to consider how you are going to transport your food and keep it cool.

Cool bags are a must, or cool boxes if your picnic location doesn't involve a hike. A box keeps things cooler for longer, protects things that need to stay upright and doubles up as an extra seat.

If you are having a posh picnic, I encourage you to take a proper hamper: the wicker ones with plates and cutlery all strapped in and a cooler sleeve for your Champers. Looking like the real deal is all part of the fun on this type of feast.

They are not the most practical but they absolutely add to the sense of occasion. Clearly you will need to take cool bags to transport the food. Same goes for the Red Riding Hood-type picnic basket. If you want to go all-out romance, this really looks the part. It's also good for carrying dishes and cutlery – just make sure you wrap them all up to stop them rattling.

Picnicking with children requires easy-life options – and this comes in the form of wheels. I have no shame whatsoever in using a pull-along-trolley, otherwise known as a 'granny shopping trolley'. It's brilliant (and why the chapter for kids is called Meals on Wheels). I can pack it with boxes of food, blankets and flasks and wheel it across the roughest of terrains. Some folk may laugh at me. I merely laugh at the amount of bags they are carrying in return.

If you are heading out on a hike or cycling, the food clearly needs to fit in a backpack. My trick is to freeze a bottle of water the night before, so it doubles up as a freezer block, keeps the food cold and gives you an extra cold drink (eventually).

CONTAINERS

Investing in a set of airtight containers is a must. If you are like me, you have a disaster area in your cupboard where they all sit, divorced from their lids. Any need for a container is accompanied by a lot of muttering about how one day I'll colour-code the lids so I can find the right one in a flash. The day never comes.

Small jam jars are perfect for simple salad dressings. See suggestions for quick and easy ones on pages 244 to 245.

Freezer bags are handy too: transporting food that doesn't need a box and bringing home leftovers. I buy decent ones with those little zip lockers and wash them out to re-use.

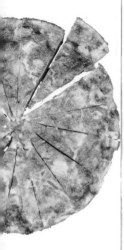

CHEAP AND CHEERFUL CROCKERY

Make yourself a collection of unbreakable melamine plates and cups. You can also get good ones made from bamboo. I am a bit of magpie when it comes to picnicware. I buy it in charity shops or supermarket sales at the end of each summer. My collection is happily mismatched, and I like watching the discussions people have about them when they get to choose a plate. Melamine serving bowls are worth investing in too – a sea of plastic tubs on a picnic blanket belies the effort and love that has gone into making the food.

This is all true unless you are doing the full posh hamper. Then anything goes. In which case, it involves as much as you are prepared to carry to set the scene: candelabras, Champagne buckets, knock yourself out.

SETTING THE SCENE

A picnic rug is essential but you've probably guessed that. Just the presence of one can make a sandwich feel special. Get a fancy one – the kind you are excited about shaking out when you find your perfect spot. An old dust sheet just won't do.

Consider a few 'special touches' to create a sense of occasion – however small. If you are trying to impress on a romantic picnic, take a teeny plastic vase and pick a flower to place in the middle of the rug or picnic table. Take strings of battery-operated fairy lights or solar lights if you're eating at dusk, and bunting hung in the tree always delights the kids and 'sets camp'.

PREPARATION AND TIPS

I'm all for the spontaneous picnic: grab a baguette, some cheese and ham and fly out the door. However, for true picnic perfection, preparation is the key. The more you do at home the better the occasion.

Get information about the picnic spot. How far is it from the car? Don't pack a huge hamper if you are scaling down a steep cliff path to get to a remote little cove. Change your food plans to suit the location.

Make the food the day before if possible, as it gives you time to cool it down and pack it.

You'll notice on the recipe pages that my use of baking parchment is pretty prolific. It helps keep slices of cake and individual pies in one piece during transit.

Don't forget to freeze the ice blocks. Pack empty cool bags or boxes with them about 3 hours before you go (it brings the temperature right down), then change them for freshly frozen ones when you pack the food. I also take frozen bottles of water to the picnic: they are good for drinks on a hot day and another supply of water for wiping fingers.

Take kitchen roll, bin bags and some form of wipe – preferably wet flannels and not those environmentally unfriendly wet wipes.

Take extra napkins or little muslin covers to keep insects off the open food containers.

Always pack an umbrella and some good old British spirit.

PICNIC SPOT
LOCATOR

BACKPACKS

1 Sandwood Bay, Kinlochbervie

2 The Wrekin, near Telford

3 Garreg Ddu Resevoir, Elan Valley

4 Catbells, Derwent Water

5 St David's Head, Pembrokeshire

6 Slippery Stones, Howden Reservoir

7 Kielder Water, Northumberland

8 Four Falls, Brecon Beacons

9 Golden Cap, Dorset

10 Alsop en le Dale, Derbyshire

ROMANTIC BASKETS

11 Loch an Eilein, Highlands

12 Brontë Falls, West Yorkshire

13 The Great Stone of Fourstones, Yorkshire

14 Padley Gorge, Peak District

15 Bedruthan Steps, Cornwall

16 Mewslade Bay & Fall Bay, Gower Peninsula

17 Llanddwyn Island, Anglesey

18 Grantchester Meadows, Cambridge

19 Fairy Pools, Isle of Skye

20 St Dunstan's Church, London

COOL BOXES

21 Heavens Gate, Wiltshire

22 Cadbury Castle, Somerset

23 Spitchwick Common, Dartmoor

24 Winterton Beach, Norfolk

25 Brockhill Country Park, Kent

26 Devils Dyke, East Sussex

27 Jephson Gardens, Warwickshire

28 Savernake Forest, Wiltshire

29 Firkin Point, Loch Lomond

30 Barricane Beach, North Devon

MEALS ON WHEELS

31 Dalby Forest, Yorkshire

32 Verulamium Park, Suffolk

33 Whisby Nature Park, Lincolnshire

34 Rumbling Kern, Northumberland

35 Ham Hill Country Park, Somerset

36 Haughmond Hill, Shropshire

37 Otters Pool, Galloway

38 Yorkshire Sculpture Park

39 Miners Welfare Park, Warwickshire

40 New Forest, Hampshire

POSH HAMPERS

41 Chatsworth Estate, Derbyshire

42 South Lawn, Surrey

43 Lily Hill Park, Berkshire

44 Fountains Abbey, North Yorkshire

45 Sheringham Park, Norfolk

46 Wollaton Park, Nottinghamshire

47 Margam Country Park, South Wales

48 Oxford Botanic Garden and Arboretum, Oxfordshire

49 Abbey Gardens, Suffolk

50 Portmeirion, Gwynedd

BARBECUES

51 Bolton Abbey, Yorkshire

52 Mersea Island, Essex

53 Yellowcraig Beach, East Lothian

54 Cardinham Woods, Cornwall

55 Rendlesham Forest, Suffolk

56 Lydiard Park, Wiltshire

57 New Forest, Hampshire

58 Ramscombe, Somerset

59 Shell Island, Gwynedd

60 Mallards Pike, Gloucestershire

1
BACKPACKS

FOR HIKERS, BIKERS AND LOVERS OF LYCRA

Travelling to a picnic spot by pedal or à pied means picnickers can get themselves to the best away-from-the-crowd spots.

I've enjoyed some of my most beautiful picnics like this, a favourite being a much needed refuelling break while hiking high up on Dartmoor. I sat with a tor as my table and not another soul in sight. It was certainly one of life's memorable meals.

These picnic snacks are perfect for being on the move: high on taste and energy, yet compact and light enough to carry neatly in your backpack. In this chapter, I've also stuck to ingredients that will fare better for longer and focused on foods that are more robust than, say, a delicate smoked fish tart or cream cake.

You'll want something that doesn't require cutlery and is generally easy to eat. Most of all, if you are serious bikers and hikers, you'll be in need of some real energy-giving foods – all of the recipes in this chapter have these things in mind.

So spend a little time in your kitchen then sling the results on your back and stroll, hike, cycle or row your own way to the perfect out-of-the-way spot for lunch.

BACON, EGG & TOMATO
RICE BARS

If adventure and endurance is your game, then energy should be your aim. These tasty savoury squares are made with sushi rice to give you a neat carbohydrate boost when you need it. The flavour comes from the salt and smokiness of the bacon, while the addition of the egg and cheese help the squares keep their shape.

Ingredients

125g sushi rice
(short grain rice)

6 slices smoky back bacon, chopped into 1cm pieces

4 spring onions, sliced

6 sun-dried tomatoes, roughly chopped

2 medium eggs

2 tsp oil, for frying

50g cheddar cheese, grated

Black pepper

20cm x 15cm rectangular dish or plastic tub, lined with cling film

Method

Rinse the rice well in a sieve then add to a saucepan with 180ml of water. Bring to the boil, then simmer for 8 to 10 minutes until the water has absorbed. If it absorbs before this time, add a little more water. Keep an eye on it, and add a little more water to prevent it evaporating completely.

Turn off the heat, keep the lid on and let it stand for about 20 minutes. Meanwhile, in a non-stick frying pan, add one teaspoon of oil and fry the bacon pieces with the spring onion. Add the sun-dried tomatoes when the bacon starts to brown slightly and heat for another minute.

In a separate bowl, beat the eggs and season with black pepper. Add the other teaspoon of oil to the pan then pour the egg mixture in.

Stir constantly as if you are making scrambled egg. As soon as it starts to solidify, add the rice and the grated cheese and stir over a low heat until the cheese has melted. This should only take a minute. Don't worry, it is meant to look a bit jumbled and sticky.

Tip the mixture into the lined dish. Push it all down really well in order to make it firm. Put into the fridge to set for at least 2 hours, longer if possible. When it has set, lift it out and cut into eight rectangles.

Stack with greaseproof paper between slices and pack tightly in a lunch box.

Prep time: 35 minutes
Cooking time: 2 hours to chill
Makes: 8 bars

CHOCOLATE, ORANGE & PINE NUT
COOKIES

I know that the rest of this chapter majors on healthy, nourishing picnic food for active picnickers but I make no apology for including my chocolate orange cookies here too. What about nourishing the soul? We all know there is nothing like a boost of chocolate when you are feeling a little bit tired.

Ingredients

225g good-quality
dark chocolate

120g unsalted butter, softened

60g light muscovado sugar

200g self-raising flour

2 tbsp good-quality
cocoa powder

3 tbsp fine-cut orange
marmalade

2 tbsp pine nuts

Zest of 1 large orange,
plus 1 tbsp of juice

Method

Preheat the oven to 180°C/Fan 160°C/350°F/Gas mark 4.

Line two baking trays with baking parchment. Divide the chocolate in half. Put one half, broken into pieces, into a heatproof bowl that can fit snugly over a saucepan of simmering water. Make sure the bowl isn't touching the water and let it melt, stirring occasionally. Roughly chop the other half of the chocolate into small pieces and put to one side.

With an electric mixer, cream together the softened butter and sugar until fluffy, then sift in the flour and the cocoa powder. Mix it well. Pour the melted chocolate into the sugar, butter and flour mixture, add the marmalade, the chopped chocolate pieces, the pine nuts, the orange zest and juice.

Gently mix it all together until well combined, taking care not to break up the chocolate pieces and pine nuts. You should end up with a sticky, glossy, dough-like mixture.

Using your hands, shape the dough into 16 balls (about the size of a walnut) and space them out on your baking trays. Make sure there is room for them to spread out when cooking.

However much you are tempted, don't skip this next bit. Put the trays in the fridge for 10 minutes before putting them into the preheated oven for 10 minutes. When cooked, leave them to stiffen up for a few minutes, then put on a cooling rack until completely cool.

Prep time: 30 minutes
Cooking time: 10 minutes
Makes: 16 cookies

BANANA & BLUEBERRY
LOAF CAKE

Okay, so here's a second recipe for nourishing the soul, rather than the body, just like the cookies on the previous page. I like my banana cake dark, rich and moist. It's worth walking or cycling an extra few miles to offset the calories of a slice of this banana and blueberry loaf cake, slathered in lots of butter.

Ingredients

2 large eggs

240g light muscovado sugar

250g ripe bananas, peeled and mashed

1 tbsp honey

280g plain flour

1 tsp baking powder

1 tsp bicarbonate of soda

1 tsp ginger

¼ tsp nutmeg

1 tsp cinnamon

140g unsalted butter, melted

3 tbsp fresh blueberries

23cm x 12cm (2lb) loaf tin, greased and lined

Method

Preheat the oven to 170°C/Fan 150°C/325°F/Gas mark 3.

Beat the eggs and sugar together until well combined. Mix in the mashed banana and honey. Combine the flour, baking powder, bicarbonate of soda, ginger, nutmeg and cinnamon in a separate bowl then add to the egg mixture and mix well until it is thoroughly blended.

Scrape the mixture down from the sides of the bowl and pour in the melted butter and beat again.

Finally, fold in the fresh blueberries, taking care not to mash them all up – you want to keep some whole.

Pour the thick batter-like mixture into the prepared loaf tin and use the back of a spoon to even out the top.

Bake in the preheated oven for about an hour, although test it after 50 minutes by pushing a skewer into the centre of the cake. If it comes out clean and the cake is springy to the touch it's ready, if not put it back in for another 5 minutes or so, and check again. Continue until your skewer comes out clean.

Leave the cake in the tin until it has cooled. Don't try to cut it before. Cut into generous slices and wrap each one in baking paper. Even better, spread a generous layer of real butter on each slice before wrapping.

Prep time: 10 minutes
Cooking time: 1 hour
Serves: 8

ENERGY BOOST GRANOLA BARS

These bars are absolutely packed with natural, energy-giving ingredients: nuts, seeds, oats and peanut butter all bound together with dates. I used to set these in the fridge without cooking, which produces a lovely chewy bar, but here I've popped them in the oven to firm them up just slightly so that they stay together better in your backpack.

Ingredients

150g stoned dates, roughly chopped

120g rolled oats

30g walnut halves, roughly chopped

15g pumpkin seeds

30g dried cranberries or cherries

70g whole almonds, roughly chopped

65g peanut butter

8 tbsp honey

½ tsp ginger

1 tsp cinnamon

Pinch of nutmeg

1 tsp vanilla essence

20cm x 20cm brownie tin

Method

Preheat the oven to 180°C/Fan 160°C/350°F/Gas mark 4.

Line the brownie tin with baking parchment.

Using a hand blender or electric mixer, blend the dates until they form a sticky ball.

Put the blended dates into a bowl and add the oats, walnuts, pumpkin seeds, cranberries (or cherries) and almonds.

In a small saucepan, gently heat together the peanut butter, honey, ginger, cinnamon, nutmeg and vanilla essence. Stir well to combine all the ingredients then pour them into the oat and date mixture and give the whole lot a really good mix.

Tip it into the prepared tin and press the mixture down firmly to make sure it is packed in well.

Put the tin into the oven for 10 minutes to lightly bake then take out and leave to cool.

Put it into the fridge for at least a couple of hours before cutting into bars.

Prep time: 10 minutes
Cooking time: 10 minutes
Makes: 12 bars

PITTA POCKETS

Pitta pockets are the most convenient way of making a picnic quickly. They are easily transportable and can pack a fabulous flavour punch. When choosing what to fill them with, I think of quirky pizza toppings or restaurant salad bowls as inspiration – here are four suggestions of what to pack in yours. Each recipe is made with two large pitta breads.

THE ROCKET POCKET

Ingredients

1 medium aubergine

2 tbsp pesto

150g soft goat's cheese

8 sun-dried tomatoes

A handful of rocket leaves

Method

Slice an aubergine into 1.5cm slices and brush both sides with oil. Fry them gently for about 20 minutes until they go beautifully soft and start to turn brown.

Cut each pitta bread in half. Spread the inside of your pitta pocket with pesto. Use a sharp knife to cut the goat's cheese into round slices, or crumble it, if easier. Put two slices of goat's cheese into each half along with four sun-dried tomatoes.

When the aubergine has cooked and cooled, put this on top of the goat's cheese and stuff some rocket leaves on top to finish it off.

THE CHICKEN CAESAR

Ingredients

1 chicken breast, cooked and shredded

1 baby gem lettuce, roughly chopped

For the dressing

3 tbsp mayonnaise

4 tinned anchovies, crushed with the back of a fork

1 tbsp lemon juice

1 small garlic clove, grated

Salt and coarsely ground black pepper

Method

Mix all of the dressing ingredients together with a small whisk.

Put the shredded chicken and lettuce into a bowl. Pour the dressing over the top and gently mix. Pack this into the pitta pockets.

Prep time: 5 to 10 minutes
Cooking time: 10 to 30 minutes
Makes: 2 large pittas per recipe

THE BFC

Ingredients

4 large carrots, scrubbed, peeled and grated

2 medium beetroots, scrubbed, topped, tailed and grated

6 radishes, sliced

150g feta cheese, cut into small cubes

A large handful of flat-leafed parsley, roughly chopped

For the dressing

Juice of ½ lemon and ½ orange

2 tbsp olive oil

Salt and black pepper

1 tbsp wholegrain mustard

1 tsp honey

1 garlic clove, finely grated

Method

Put the grated carrot, beetroot and radish slices in a bowl. Separately mix the dressing by whisking all the ingredients together, then pour over the vegetables. Add the cubes of feta to the bowl along with the parsley.

Mix it gently to make sure the dressing coats all the cheese and vegetables. I find using my hands is best.

Leave for about 30 minutes to let the flavours infuse before packing the mix into the pittas.

THE NEW YORKER

Ingredients

6 slices pastrami, or other deli ham of your choice

3 large gherkins, sliced

4 slices emmental cheese

For the dressing

1 tbsp mayonnaise

1 tbsp horseradish sauce

½ tbsp ketchup

Method

Mix the dressing ingredients together, then layer pastrami, dressing, cheese and gherkin, and repeat, into the pockets.

BACKPACK BURRITOS

These meat-free sandwich wraps are packed with Mexican-inspired flavours of chilli, limes and avocados, and the black beans and quinoa will give you plenty of energy. The wraps can be assembled in under 30 minutes, or if you want to set off early in the morning, cook the quinoa the night before and keep it in the fridge.

Ingredients

150g quinoa

1 tsp stock powder

1 small red onion, finely chopped

1 tbsp olive oil

1 garlic clove, finely grated

1 tsp cumin

½ tsp ground coriander

200g tinned black beans, drained and rinsed

200g sweetcorn

1 lime, cut in half

A large bunch of fresh coriander leaves, chopped

4 fresh tomatoes, deseeded and flesh roughly chopped

½ red chilli, deseeded and finely chopped

2 large avocados, stoned and the flesh roughly chopped

100g feta or cheddar cheese

4 flour tortillas

Method

Cook the quinoa in a saucepan of boiling water with the stock powder (about 20 to 25 minutes). Drain and leave in the sieve while making the rest of the filling.

Heat the oil in a frying pan and fry the onion for 5 minutes, then add the garlic, cumin and ground coriander, and stir until the onion is coated with the spices.

Add the black beans and sweetcorn, heat through and then add the drained quinoa with the juice of half of the lime and half the chopped coriander and heat gently.

In a separate bowl, combine the chopped tomato, the avocado, the finely sliced chilli, the rest of the coriander and the other half of the lime juice. Add the quinoa mixture and gently combine so as not to mush the avocado.

Lay the tortilla wraps on squares of foil laid out on a work surface and divide the mixture equally between them. Top each of them with grated cheese.

Roll the burritos tightly and wrap in foil, twisting the ends to keep the mixture securely in the wraps while you transport them.

Once you have found your picnic spot, cut (or firmly tear) the wraps in half and peel the foil off as you eat them.

Prep time: 10 minutes
Cooking time: 30 minutes
Makes: 4 wraps

ALI'S SCRUMPTIOUS
PICNIC LOAF

Half sandwich, half pie, this picnic loaf crams the best of the deli counter into one easy-to-carry meal. The great thing about this is that you can chop and change the ingredients according to the flavours you like and what is available in the fridge. Prepare it the night before so the flavours have time to develop.

Ingredients

1 medium-sized cob loaf
(the crusty round one)

2 small red and 2 small yellow peppers, sliced in thick lengths (or use pre-roasted marinated peppers from a 450g jar)

1 garlic clove, cut in half

3 tbsp pesto

100g sun-dried tomatoes, drained

2 tbsp capers

200g cheese, sliced – either mozzarella, brie, goat's cheese or a combination

200g charcuterie meats or ham

A bag of mixed salad leaves (approx 100g)

A handful of fresh basil leaves

Olive oil

Salt and black pepper

Measurements are a guide for a 400g loaf. Adapt them depending on the shape and size of cob loaf you use

Method

Carefully cut the top off the cob bread (save this for later) and hollow out the middle of the loaf to leave the shell (don't make the walls too thin as it won't stay crisp).

If using fresh peppers, toss the slices in the olive oil and put into a hot griddle pan. Cook for 4 to 5 minutes on each side until soft and lightly charred. Blot with kitchen paper to get the excess oil off and put to one side. If using roasted peppers from a jar, you will also need to dry them with kitchen paper. Do the same with the sun-dried tomatoes and capers.

Rub the cut garlic clove over the inside of the bread shell before using the back of a spoon to spread the pesto all around the inside walls, and under the lid.

Season the peppers and slices of mozzarella (if using) with salt and pepper, then start building up layers of peppers, capers, sun-dried tomatoes, cheese, meat and leaves until the hollowed space is tightly packed. You'll have to really push the ingredients down to get a dense filling. Finish with a layer of basil leaves.

Put the top of the bread back on and wrap tightly in cling film. Then put a plate on top and weigh the loaf down with something like a book for at least 2 hours, preferably overnight, in the fridge. Cut into thick, cake-style slices to wrap individually with cling film to pack in your lunch box.

Prep time: 30 minutes
Cooking time: 2 hours to chill
Serves: 4

SWEET POTATO & CHEDDAR
MUFFINS

Sweet potato is full of slow-release, energy-giving carbohydrates and makes a great base for these savoury muffins. They are a little wild looking as I've grated the potato not mashed it, but I think rustic suits the adventurous occasion of an active picnic. Once tasted, these gorgeously gooey, sticky, savoury muffins will become a favourite.

Ingredients

300g sweet potato, peeled

125g self-raising flour

½ tsp baking powder

2 springs onions, finely sliced

1 tbsp chives, finely chopped

30g cheddar cheese, finely grated, plus extra for the top

½ tsp Chinese five spice

1 tbsp pumpkin seeds, plus extra for decoration

2 large eggs, beaten

2 tbsp crème fraîche

Salt and black pepper

Method

Preheat the oven to 180°C/Fan 160°C/350°F/Gas mark 4.

Prepare eight cups of a muffin tin with muffin cases or folded squares of greaseproof paper, brushed with a little oil, pushed into the muffin spaces.

Grate the potato into a bowl. Sift the flour and baking powder into the bowl and mix it all together so the potato is coated with the flour. Add the spring onions, chives, cheese, Chinese five spice, pumpkin seeds, and a seasoning of salt and pepper and mix it all together.

Beat the eggs and crème fraîche in another bowl then pour it into the bowl with the potato, then stir it all together thoroughly. It will look a bit lumpy but that's fine.

Divide the mixture evenly between the cases and sprinkle a few extra pumpkin seeds and a small amount of grated cheese on the top.

Bake on the bottom shelf of the oven for about 30 to 35 minutes until golden. Push a toothpick into one to check that the mixture has cooked thoroughly, if not, put back into the oven for another 5 minutes.

Prep time: 20 minutes
Cooking time: 35 minutes
Makes: 8 muffins

SPICY
SCOTCH EGGS

This has to be one of my favourite recipes in this book. A Scotch egg is such a pleasing picnic classic, but this one has a few twists. The hint of chilli will raise an eyebrow or two and I've coated it in oatmeal rather than breadcrumbs for that all important energy release from oats and I also think it makes a better, crunchier coating than breadcrumbs.

Ingredients

6 medium eggs

400g good-quality pork sausages (or plain sausage meat)

4 tbsp chopped fresh herbs, such as sage, parsley and chives

½ large red chilli (about 5cm), deseeded and very finely chopped

1 tbsp English mustard

Salt and black pepper

2 tbsp milk

100g plain flour

150g medium oatmeal

Vegetable oil for deep frying

Method

Put four of the eggs into a large saucepan and cover with cold water. Bring to the boil. Once the water has started to boil, turn the heat down so that the eggs simmer for 4 minutes exactly. Boil for 5 minutes if you want a totally set egg.

Take the eggs out and put them straight into a bowl of cold or iced water to stop them cooking.

Using a sharp knife, split the skins on the sausages. Remove and discard the skins and put the meat into a bowl and add the chopped herbs, chilli and mustard, then season well with salt and pepper. Mix together well and divide into four equal pieces, then roll into tight balls.

Peel the cooled eggs. Lay a large sheet of cling film on a work surface and lightly dust it with flour. Put a ball of sausage meat on the top. Lightly dust with flour then lay another piece of cling film on top. Roll out the meat until it is just large enough to wrap around an egg – don't roll it too thinly.

Remove the top sheet of the cling film. Roll an egg in flour, then lay it on the rolled sausage meat. Wrap the meat around the egg and press the edges together to seal it all in. Use your hands to mould it well around the egg and make it smooth, and to really seal the edges. Chill in the fridge for 20 minutes. ➤→

Prep time: 20 minutes
Cooking time: 20 minutes
Serves: 4

SPICY
SCOTCH EGGS

➤➤ Prepare three dishes in a row. In one, beat the two remaining eggs with the milk. In another put the flour and the last put the oatmeal.

Roll the Scotch eggs in the flour, then the egg, then the oatmeal, back in the egg and finally in the oatmeal once more to get it thoroughly coated.

Fill a small to medium saucepan with enough oil to cover the egg and heat. If you have a jam thermometer to put in the oil it should be 170°C, or until a small piece of bread, dropped into the pan, sizzles and quickly turns a golden colour. Caution: don't overfill with oil or leave unattended.

Deep fry the Scotch eggs two at a time for 8 minutes or until they are crispy, deep golden in colour and cooked through.

Remove them with a slotted spoon and put into a bowl lined with kitchen paper to soak up the excess oil.

When they have cooled, wrap them in clean kitchen paper and baking parchment for transportation.

MENU IDEAS

1 **Bacon, egg and tomato rice bars | Sweet potato and cheddar muffins | Energy boost granola bars | Orange zest brownies**
Try this menu if you are in need of a constant yet steady release of energy.

2 **Backpack burritos | Energy boost granola bars | Feta, courgette, pea and mint frittata | Banana and blueberry loaf cake | Chocolate, orange and pine nut cookies**
For a hill climb, keep it lightweight but heavy on energy and some sweet rewards when you get to the top.

3 **Pitta pockets | Spicy Scotch eggs | Sweet potato and cheddar muffins | Raspberry and orange oat bites**
For taking it slower on a long stroll – with a few stops along the way and on a bench, if you are lucky.

4 **Picnic loaf | Spicy Scotch eggs | Orzo primavera salad | Chocolate, orange and pine nut cookies**
For when the weight of your backpack is less of a problem, like when you are messing about on the river.

MARVELLOUS PLACES
FOR THE
PERFECT ENERGETIC PICNIC

—— SANDWOOD BAY ——

KINLOCHBERVIE, NORTH SCOTLAND

This is the most northwesterly beach in mainland Britain, possibly the most remote, and surely the most unspoilt. When the sun shines you could be forgiven for thinking you had arrived in paradise. Here you'll find soft white sand, the bluest seas and hardly anyone else.

It's not an easy spot to get to but if you like a decent walk then a picnic on this beach will reward your efforts. Pick a spot snuggled down in the marram grass dunes if the wind gets up.

It is a fairly long walk to the beach from the car park (about 4.5 miles each way) on a clearly marked path, and there are a couple of areas where you need to use stepping stones to cross shallow water. When you arrive, take your shoes off and walk across the powdery sand that stretches a mile and a half wide. Gazing out to sea you'll see the impressive Am Buachaille sandstone sea stack, which looks like an old sailing ship heading to shore, and behind the dunes is a freshwater loch full of trout. Take your pick of perfection and soak up one of the loveliest beaches in the country.

FIND IT The nearest car park is located at Blairmore, west of Kinlochbervie, and has a box for donations to the John Muir trust. The start of the walk to the beach is clearly signposted over the road from the car park. Nearest postcode is IV27 4RU.

—— THE WREKIN ——

NR TELFORD, SHROPSHIRE

You will have certainly earned the contents of your backpack picnic once you have climbed the three and a half miles to the summit of The Wrekin. This 407-metre high mound is on the edge of the Shropshire Hills Area of Outstanding Natural Beauty and rises up out of the otherwise flat Severn Plain.

The path takes you through oak, holly and birch woodland, a delight in bluebell season and when the primroses cover the ground. On a clear day at the summit, you can picnic while enjoying the view of 17 counties. There is a topographic stone map at the top to show you what you are looking at.

While you eat, you can ponder the fact that the inhabitants of the Iron Age fort that graced this summit thousands of years ago would have gazed upon the same landscapes.

FIND IT You can see the Wrekin from miles around. There are a few routes to the summit; the most popular involves parking at Forest Glen car park to the north of the hill (Shropshire Wildlife Trust car park) and follow the path. Nearest postcode is TF6 5AL.

GARREG DDU RESEVOIR

ELAN VALLEY TRAIL, POWYS, WALES

The Elan Valley is fondly known as the 'Welsh Lake District' and boasts a spectacular cycling trail from which to choose a picnic spot. Climb past three reservoirs in the heart of beautiful, mountainous mid-Wales, following the line of the old Birmingham Corporation Railway. You'll reach Garreg Ddu Resevoir and its stunning views of the surrounding valleys. It's a fabulous place to stop and refuel with a backdrop of Victorian dams and reservoirs and expansive open hills.

For all its beauty, it doesn't draw the hoards like the Brecon Beacons do, so you will find a good dose of peace and quiet here. The trail is also right in the heart of red kite country – look out for these splendid birds with their distinctive forked tails riding the thermals above you as you enjoy a rest on the rug.

FIND IT The trail starts from the pretty community of Cwmdeuddwr to the western side of the large town of Rhayader (there is plenty of parking in Rhayader). The marked trail climbs up over the Rhayadar tunnel (home to a colony of bats). Push on past the spectacular dams and reservoirs to reach the Garreg Ddu Resevoir. It's 16 miles there and back.

CATBELLS

DERWENT WATER, CUMBRIA

For a rug with a view, you can't go wrong with heading up Catbells Hill in the Lake District for a spectacular vista over Derwent Water and Keswick. Leaving from Manesty near Grange, it's a great beginners' fell walk as it delivers 100 per cent on the scenery without being as high as some of the other Lake District classics.

Wherever you decide to stop to open the backpack, you'll be treated to a view better than any restaurant could ever offer you. You'll see some of the key Lake District sights from here: Bassenthwaite Lake, Skiddaw and Keswick on the north shore of Derwent Water.

But that's not all, as you are looking at the settings for some of Beatrix Potter's most loved stories. Below you is the real life town of Little Town of Mrs Tiggy-Winkle fame and Catbells Hill features in the stories as Mrs Tiggy-Winkle's home.

FIND IT There is parking for 10 cars at the base of the ridge at Hawkes Head, however you can leave the car in the village of Grange (just off the B5289) and walk westwards out of the village towards Manesty. You'll pass the Borrowdale Gates Hotel on your right. Stay on the lane until just after Manesty. Turn left and begin the climb, ignoring the path that heads off to the right. When you reach Hause Gate, turn right and you will be on the ridge path to the summit.

—— ST DAVID'S HEAD ——

PEMBROKESHIRE, WALES

A hike on the extremities of St David's Head in Pembrokeshire is full of otherworldliness. You are thrust out on a limb, leaving modern concerns behind as you pass through a landscape heaving with myths, legends and the ancient past.

Setting off from the spectacular surfing mecca that is Whitesands Bay, you can walk the loop around St David's Head and experience what has been described as the most mystical place in Wales. There is so much evidence of ancient civilisation here that you could trip over it. Clawdd-y-Milwyr, the Warriors Dyke, was an immense wall constructed by Iron Age farmers here – for what we don't know. You'll spot the remains of the wall scattered among the wildflowers.

Stop to eat by Arthur's Quoit, an enormous stone slab held upright by a thin stone to mark the entrance of a 6,000-year-old burial chamber. Alternatively, push on for the rocky summit, Carn Llidi (595ft) passing two more burial chambers. Sitting at the top will give you a spectacular view of the coastline and a seascape scattered with islands.

FIND IT Just a few miles out of St David's, leave the car at Whitesands beach car park (postcode is SA62 6PS). From the car park, go through a gap in the wall on passing the site of St Patrick's Chapel. Climb a sandy slope up on to the cliff path.

—— SLIPPERY STONES ——

HOWDEN RESERVOIR, PEAK DISTRICT

A ten-mile walk or cycle ride around Derwent and Howden reservoirs should build up an appetite for a picnic. A fabulous place to stop is halfway round, a spot known as Slippery Stones. It is favoured by wild swimmers, so you might want to pack your cozzie if it's a warm day. Sit on the grass bank next to the stream and watch the ducks against a backdrop of an old stone pack horse bridge and the hills of the Peak District beyond. It is a peaceful spot, away from traffic and feels suitably wild and away from it all.

FIND IT Park at Fairholmes visitor centre, Bamford, Hope Valley, S33 0AQ, and either walk or cycle the track up to King's Tree. Follow the main path until the cycle way turns right up a hill, cross the small wooden bridge and follow the grassy path left until you reach the plunge pool. It is possible to drive up the track to King's Tree from the visitor centre on weekdays but closed to traffic at weekends. There is cycle hire at the visitor centre.

—— KIELDER WATER ——

NORTHUMBLAND

Europe's largest man-made reservoir also lays claim to some of the darkest night skies in the country, as there is no light pollution. It's also been scientifically proven to be the quietest place in the country due to its distance away from flight paths and roads. With such a list of superlatives, this surely has to be one of the most perfect places for an outdoor feast.

If you like a decent walk there are lots of options for great spots to stop and eat. Many people visit the park for the open air art experience. There are a series of evocative art installations placed in the forest and around the water's edge. You could settle in one of the three large rotating Janus Chairs that offer shelter and a view of Kielder Water, or the very popular Silvas Capitalis, also known as the giant forest head. It's made out of timber and is big enough for people to walk inside.

Another secretive spot for rest and refreshment is Patterson's Pause at Lewisburn inlet, a cove within the forest's most secluded valley. A short climb from the Lewisburn suspension bridge is the stone block table and chairs of Patterson's Pause. It's a tranquil location with a beautiful view, often shared with herons and buzzards, overlooking the secluded and peaceful waters of Lewisburn inlet.

FIND IT Kielder Water is about 30 miles from Hexham and Jedburgh.

—— FOUR FALLS ——

YSTRADFELLTE, BRECON BEACONS, WALES

Nestled into the southern slopes of the Fforest Fawr massif, west of Merthyr Tydfil, 'Waterfall Country' is one of the most beautiful and popular parts of the Brecon Beacons National Park, as it has the greatest concentration of cascades, caves and gorges anywhere in Britain. Head on the Four Falls walk for a hike through the steep, tree-lined gorges and you'll find many places to stop and eat to the soothing soundtrack of tumbling water.

The village of Ystradfellte is the starting point. From the car park, the river next to the path is swallowed completely by the Porth yr Ogof cave at one point, only to be found further along rushing out of the hillside towards the waterfalls. There are four waterfalls along here, of which, Sgwd yr Eira is a wide horse-shoe shape and has a ledge behind it that you can walk on to and experience the thrill of standing behind the rush of water as it cascades over the ledge. Choose a suitable tree trunk as your picnic bench.

FIND IT The walk begins in Cwm Porth car park (nearest postcode is CF44 9JE) that sits directly above the entrance to the Porth yr Ogof cave system. You can reach the car park by following signs along minor roads from the village of Ystradfellte.

—— GOLDEN CAP ——

SOUTH COAST, DORSET

The effort of walking the South West Coast Path is rewarded with the soul-stirring vistas of the rugged coastline along the way. It's a little like hiking a rollercoaster track, and one of the most thrilling dips and peak is Golden Cap. The views from this spot on the path between Lyme Regis and Bridport are truly spectacular. The honey-hued rock of the Jurassic Coast (the only Natural World Heritage Site in England) stretches out into the distance. It is especially beautiful late on a sunny day when the sun makes it glow.

Golden Cap has plentiful grassy spots between the bracken, heather, bilberry and bramble to sit, rest and replete. Be sensible about placing your picnic blanket a little way back from the cliff edge though; instead you can watch the brave wild rabbits who seem to dare each other to go as close to the edge as possible.

FIND IT Park in the car park by the beach at Seatown, opposite the Anchor Pub. Seatown is clearly marked from the A35 down a single track road. The main car park is to your left as you reach the bottom of the hill (nearest postcode is DT6 6JU). Park then walk back up the road just beyond the caravan park and cross a stile on the left, onto the footpath, signed 'Coast Path Diversion'. Follow this until you see the sign for Golden Cap. You can see where you need to head from there.

—— ALSOP EN LE DALE ——

DERBYSHIRE DALES

Sling a meal in your backpack for a day on the bike in the Peaks. Take the 13-mile Tissington Trail (Sustrans route 68) that runs between Parsley Hay and Ashbourne. Following the route of the former Ashbourne railway line, this glorious cycle ride passes through the verdant countryside of the Derbyshire Dales. Halfway along the traffic-free route, it passes under the A515 and reaches a car park, just off which you will find a winding narrow lane to take you to a perfect lunch stop. Alsop en le Dale is a charmingly picturesque English hamlet: a cluster of houses, a handsome Elizabethan hall and a lovely church, plus a designated picnic site with some tables. It's an oasis of peace and tranquillity off the beaten track to refuel.

FIND IT If you are cycling or walking the Tissington Trail, park your car in Parsley Hay. The picnic spot in Alsop en le Dale can be found halfway along the trail, passing Alsop. The trail runs under the A515 and past a car park. Come off the trail and follow a narrow lane to the pretty hamlet.

2

ROMANTIC
BASKETS

FOR LOVERS, ROMANTICS AND DATING OUTDOORS

Good old-fashioned romance and picnics go hand-in-hand. There are many reasons to choose a picnic over sitting opposite each other at a restaurant table surrounded by strangers. For one, the natural world around you is the perfect conversation starter: the view, the activities on the lake in front of you, the seagull stealing your sandwich – it adds memories to the occasion.

A simple impromptu picnic with your partner can be the perfect pause in an otherwise hectic existence. Taking a rug and a flask of soup in a local beauty spot can set right so much more than another quickly scoffed meal at the table.

The recipes in this chapter cover many bases. There are sharing platters (a great way to test any relationship), things that are mess-free and easy to eat such as dips and sticks, decadent boozy fruit jellies and a stunning rich chocolate cake in a made-for-two size.

Whether you are on a first date or just fancy making a special effort for your loved one, the following pages should ignite your passion for a picnic.

SMOKED
CHEESE STRAWS

This is a grown-up version of a cheese straw. They are quick and easy to make as the recipe uses shop-bought puff pastry (come on, who on earth has time to make their own puff pastry?). Use the ready-rolled version to make life even easier.

Ingredients

200g ready-rolled puff pastry

150g smoked cheese, finely grated, plus 3 extra tsp for finishing

1 tsp dried mixed herbs

Method

Preheat the oven to 220°C/Fan 200°C/425°F/Gas mark 7.

Lay the sheet of puff pastry onto a piece of baking parchment.

Mix the dried herbs with the grated cheese, then sprinkle the mixture on one of the long halves of the rectangle, and fold the plain pastry side over on top of it, so you have a rectangle with a layer of cheese in the middle.

Place another piece of baking parchment over the top and use a rolling pin to roll it flat, keeping the rectangle shape as much as possible. Make sure the cheese is well and truly pushed into the pastry. You want to roll it out enough that you've increased its folded size by roughly a third.

Use a sharp knife to trim the edges to get a neat rectangle then cut the rectangle into 12 strips of about 1cm. Lift the baking parchment onto a baking tray and spread the strips out a little.

Carefully sprinkle the remaining cheese over the top of each straw. I like to twist the pastry straws at this point so they cook in a spiral but it's up to you if you go twisty or straight.

Bake in the hot oven for 9 to 10 minutes. They should be a nice golden brown colour.

Leave to cool on the tray for 10 minutes before removing carefully with a spatula or fish slice. They are quite fragile, so pack in your picnic box between sheets of kitchen paper.

Prep time: 10 minutes
Cooking time: 10 minutes
Makes: 12 straws

SHARING PLATTER

Many years ago on my honeymoon in Italy, I chose a starter off a menu with no English translation. A simple plate of figs, manchego cheese drizzled in honey and a scattering of juniper berries arrived. It is a plate of food I will never forget. I've included a similar set of flavours here because I was in love when I ate that dish, and this is a picnic for lovers.

Ingredients

8 ripe figs

150g manchego cheese

4 tbsp walnut pieces

100ml gin

2 tbsp honey

80g prosciutto, about 8 slices

Method

Preheat the oven to 200°C/Fan 180°C/400°F/Gas mark 6.

Twist the stalks off the figs and cut a deep cross down into each one. Squeeze the sides of the figs to expose the pink flesh.

Nestle them into a baking dish (you want them touching not rolling about the dish) with the crossed side upwards.

Carefully pour the gin onto the fleshy parts of the figs, push some walnut pieces into the crosses and then drizzle honey over the top.

Cover with foil or a lid and bake in the oven for about 15 minutes.

Allow to cool and pack the figs (pouring the cooking juices over them) in a tub for your picnic.

When you are ready to serve, arrange the figs on a wooden board, alongside the slices of manchego cheese, slices of prosciutto and a handful of walnut pieces. Drizzle a little extra honey over the manchego slices then sit back and see how good your date is at sharing.

Try a hard goat's cheese instead of the manchego

Prep time: 10 minutes
Cooking time: 15 minutes
Serves: 2

SMOKY
AUBERGINE DIP

Silky in texture and smoky on the palate – this is a mellow melt-in-the-mouth dip. It is a twist on my favourite aubergine dip, the Middle Eastern baba ganoush. Usually, the aubergines are blackened in a flame or grilled to get a very smoky flavour. However, this method is easier as it roasts them in the oven, which still gives a deliciously smoky hit.

Ingredients

500g aubergines

1 tbsp mild olive oil, plus more for brushing the aubergine

2 tbsp tahini

1 large garlic clove, skin on

2 tbsp lemon juice

A pinch of seasalt flakes and coarsely ground black pepper

To serve

1 tsp sweet smoked paprika

2 tsp olive oil, plus more for the pittas

2 tbsp fresh flat parsley, chopped

4 pitta breads

Method

Preheat the oven to 200°C/Fan 180°C/400°F/Gas mark 6.

Cut the tops off the aubergines and peel them. Slice them thickly and brush both sides with olive oil, making sure they are properly coated. Coat the garlic clove in olive oil.

Roast the aubergine and garlic in the oven for about 20 minutes until the aubergines turn soft and start to go brown, but not crispy.

Let the slices cool until you can handle them and put them in a food processor. Squeeze the soft garlic clove out of its skin and add to the aubergine along with the tahini and the lemon juice.

Blitz it all together until it is creamy and silky. Have a taste and add more lemon juice according to your tastes and season well with salt and pepper.

Mix the paprika with the olive oil to make a bright red runny paste and keep in a small container.

When you are ready to serve, drizzle it over the dip in a swirl (or a love heart shape) and sprinkle chopped parsley over the top.

For the pittas, use kitchen scissors to cut them into wedges, brush both sides of the wedges with olive oil and spread on a baking tray. Bake in the oven for 5 minutes, turn them over and give them another 3 minutes until they have turned golden brown and crispy. Let them cool before packing in an air-tight tub.

Best eaten on the day it's made

Prep time: 15 minutes
Cooking time: 30 minutes
Serves: 2

SMOKED SALMON & ASPARAGUS TARTLETS

A refined tartlet is the perfect main event for a picnic à deux. The asparagus complements the smoked salmon beautifully, and there's an added little kick of heat from the dash of horseradish. This recipe makes six individual tartlets, and they freeze really well so you can keep the rest for the next date.

Ingredients

400g shop-bought shortcrust pastry, or see recipe on page 247

Filling

12 fine asparagus stems

2 medium eggs

2 medium egg yolks

200ml double cream

1 tbsp horseradish sauce

1 tbsp lemon juice

Salt and black pepper

80g smoked salmon, cut into 1cm pieces

4 tsp finely grated parmesan

6 individual, loose-bottom, non-stick 10cm diameter x 2.5cm tartlet tins

Method

Preheat the oven to 180°C/Fan 160°C/350°F/Gas mark 4.

Divide the pastry equally into six and roll out thinly (it is easier to do this between two sheets of cling film), and line the tartlet tins. Blind bake the pastry by pricking the base with a fork, then pushing a square of baking parchment into the case and weighing down the parchment with ceramic baking beads or dry lentils.

Bake for 10 minutes, remove the beads and parchment, then put back into the oven for 5 minutes to lightly brown the bases.

Turn the oven down to 170°C/Fan 150°C/325°F/Gas mark 3.

To make the filling, cut the asparagus into 7cm pieces – you want 12 tips of 7cm to fit into your tins. The other pieces can be used in the orza salad on page 60. Put the tips into a bowl of boiling water for about 4 minutes just to soften them slightly.

Beat the eggs and egg yolks with the cream, horseradish and lemon juice, with a seasoning of salt and pepper. Divide the salmon pieces between the tartlets and carefully pour over the egg and cream mixture. Top them with a couple of asparagus spears arranged in a cross and sprinkle parmesan cheese over the top of each one.

Bake for 25 minutes. Check the centres are just cooked, wobbly is good, liquid is not. It might need another minute or so. Leave to cool before turning out of the tartlet tins and packing carefully with lots of greaseproof paper to protect them.

Prep time: 20 minutes
Cooking time: 40 minutes
Makes: 6 tartlets

ORZO
PRIMAVARA SALAD

This is a summery pasta salad of fresh seasonal vegetables. Orzo is the tiny rice-shaped pasta – you can use other pasta, but I feel the orzo keeps this dish nice and light. I've made a zesty dressing and used plentiful fresh herbs. The amount here is for the salad as a main serving, though it would go well with the salmon tartlets.

Ingredients

200g orzo pasta

150g courgette

300g fresh broad beans in their shells, or approx 80g podded

150g frozen peas

100g asparagus, cut into 3cm lengths (use stalks from salmon tartlets)

1 tbsp fresh mint leaves, chopped

1 tbsp fresh parsley, chopped

A handful of parmesan shavings (optional)

Dressing

1 tsp unwaxed lemon zest

2 tbsp lemon juice

1 tsp Dijon mustard

4 tbsp olive or rapeseed oil

½ garlic clove, finely grated

1 tsp sugar

½ tsp salt

Coarsely ground black pepper

Method

Cook the orzo according to packet instructions. Turn off the heat and immediately drain and rinse with cold water. Add a teaspoon of olive or rapeseed oil and stir it through to prevent it sticking together. Tip into the bowl or tub you are going to transport it in, keep the lid off and allow to cool.

Cut the courgette into bite-sized pieces, then blanch them with the broad beans, peas and asparagus by tipping them into a pan of salted boiling water (a sprinkle of salt is enough), and letting them boil for 3 minutes, no more. Drain immediately and plunge the vegetables into a bowl of cold water. Add a few ice cubes, if possible. This stops them cooking and keeps their shape. Once they are cool, drain the vegetables and put to one side.

In a small bowl whisk together all the dressing ingredients.

Now assemble your salad, adding two tablespoons of dressing to the orzo and tossing it all together, next add the vegetables and add the rest of the dressing (according to your taste) and toss it again. Add the fresh mint, parsley and the shavings of parmesan cheese (if using) and give it a final gentle mix.

Put the lid on and pack in a cool bag.

Try swapping the asparagus for fine green beans or the broad beans for edamame

Prep time: 10 minutes
Cooking time: 20 minutes
Serves: 2

BOOZY FRUIT JELLIES

Easy on the eye and a little bit boozy, these jars of fruity jelly feel just naughty enough.

Ingredients

70g raspberry jelly, broken up into cubes

200ml mini bottle Prosecco, Champagne or Cava

100g mixed summer berries, such as strawberries, raspberries, blackcurrants and blackberries, hulled and halved if necessary

Fresh mint leaves, to decorate

2 x 250ml jam jars – ideally those ones with the pretty gingham patterned lids

Method

Put the jelly cubes in a jug, pour over 85ml of boiling water and stir until the jelly has dissolved.

Let it cool then slowly stir in the Prosecco or the alcohol of your choice.

Divide the berries between the jam jars and pour enough jelly in to just cover the fruit.

Cover and chill in the fridge until the surface is just set, which will take about 30 minutes. This helps to stop the fruit all bobbing to the top. Then top up with the remaining liquid jelly in the jug. Cover and chill for a good couple of hours until fully set.

Put a couple of fresh mint leaves on the top of the jelly then pop the lids on.

Keep them in the cool bag until you are ready to serve.

Prep time: 10 minutes
Cooking time: 2.5 hours to chill
Serves: 2

STRAWBERRY
TARTS

They just look right to take on a romantic picnic, don't they? Strawberries look like gorgeous cartoon love hearts so make sure you get some properly ripe ones for the perfect loved-up picnic. While you clearly don't need eight to take with you, I guarantee you'll eat at least four before you get out of the door. They are utterly delicious.

Ingredients

375g pack all-butter sweet shortcrust pastry, or see recipe on page 247

4 egg yolks

60g caster sugar

25g plain flour

2 tsp cornflour

250ml whole milk

1 tsp vanilla essence

8 strawberries

9cm pastry cutter and a tart tray

Method

To make the crème pâtissière, whisk the egg yolks with the sugar until it is glossy and slightly foamy. Sift in the plain and corn flours, and whisk again.

Separately, heat the milk and vanilla essence in a small saucepan. Stir it continuously to stop it burning, turn the heat down and add the egg mixture. Continue to stir whilst it is on the heat until the sauce starts to thicken a little. Take it off the heat and continue to stir for another 30 seconds to make sure the sauce is thoroughly silky. Pour in a bowl, cover with cling film and allow to cool.

Preheat the oven to 190°C/Fan 170°C/375°F/Gas mark 5.

Put the pastry on a floured surface and push it down with your hand to flatten a little. Place some cling film over the top and roll it out to 0.5cm thick. Cut out rounds and put them in a lightly floured tart tray.

Put the tart tray in the freezer (or fridge) for 15 minutes to firm up the pastry. Line each case with a circle of baking parchment and pour in some rice or baking beans. Put the tray in the oven for 15 minutes. Take it out, remove the beans and the baking parchment and pop it back in the oven for another 5 minutes. By this time they will be turning a little golden in colour and be nice and crisp. Leave them to cool completely.

When the pastry cases and the custard are cold, spoon the custard into each of the pastry cases, enough to fill them up. Cut your strawberries to look like hearts and decorate the tops.

Prep time: 40 minutes
Cooking time: 20 minutes
Makes: 8 tarts

PARSNIP & SQUASH SOUP

Picnics aren't just for summer, especially when it's a picnic for two. There is something very romantic about huddling together, wrapped in blankets against the elements. Keep things simple – take a flask of homemade soup and a crusty loaf to tear and share. Here, I've used root vegetables with a fiery kick of ginger.

Ingredients

1 tsp olive oil

1 knob butter

1 medium onion, finely chopped

2 garlic cloves, peeled and grated

3cm piece fresh ginger, grated

¼ red chilli, finely chopped

½ tsp cumin

800ml vegetable stock

300g butternut squash, peeled and cut into 2cm cubes

300g parsnips, peeled, topped, tailed and cut into 2cm cubes

Salt and black pepper

200ml milk

Method

Heat the oil and butter together in a large saucepan and fry the onion on a low heat for about 10 minutes until it softens.

Add the garlic, ginger, red chilli and cumin, and stir while it cooks for another two minutes.

Add the stock, butternut squash and parsnip cubes, season well with salt and pepper and bring to the boil. Once it starts boiling, turn the heat down to a rigorous simmer for 15 minutes until the butternut squash and parsnips have softened.

Leave it to cool a little, then use a hand blender to purée the contents of the pan. Make sure you get all of the lumps out to achieve a lovely silky smooth consistency.

Put the pan back on a low heat and add the milk. Heat it very gently while stirring continuously to blend it all together. If it looks too thick just add a little more milk to achieve the consistency you prefer.

When it is hot enough to serve, use a jug to decant into a thermos flask or insulated cups and put the lid on immediately. The amounts given here will make four generous portions so you can freeze what you don't use.

Take a couple of bowls, spoons, some hunks of cheese and rustic bread to serve.

Prep time: 15 minutes
Cooking time: 30 minutes
Serves: 2

RICH ROMANTIC
CHOCOLATE CAKE FOR TWO

If you need to pull out all the stops to impress, this beautiful chocolate cake will do it. Made in the perfect size for two, it's a declaration that it's all about the two of you – to be shared with nobody else. Yes, you will need to find yourself a small cake tin, but surely they're worth it?

Ingredients

115g unsalted butter, at room temperature

115g caster sugar

85g self-raising flour

25g cocoa powder

½ tsp baking powder

2 medium eggs

½ tsp good-quality instant coffee granules

70g dark chocolate

3 tbsp double cream

30g raspberries

A handful of blueberries

1 tsp icing sugar

15cm loose-bottom, round cake tin, greased and lined

Method

Preheat the oven to 180°C/Fan 160°C/350°F/Gas mark 4.

Use an electric mixer to beat together the butter with the caster sugar until soft and fluffy. Sieve the self-raising flour, cocoa powder and baking powder into the mixture, add the eggs and mix together again. Add the coffee and mix through once more.

Spoon the mixture into the cake tin and bake in the centre of the oven for 40 to 45 minutes. Insert a skewer to check it's cooked – it should come out clean. Place on a wire cooling rack and allow to cool.

To make the topping, put the chocolate, broken into pieces, in a heatproof bowl set over a pan of boiling water, making sure the bottom of the bowl doesn't touch the water. Stir until it melts.

Pour the melted chocolate into a bowl with the double cream and mix well until it is thoroughly combined and glossy. Spread over the top of the cake loosely and thickly with a knife, not quite reaching the edges.

Put the raspberries and blueberries in a small dish and sprinkle with icing sugar. Mix very gently and let the icing sugar absorb into the fruit. Place the fruit on top of the cake.

Make the sponge the day before and keep it in the fridge

Prep time: 30 minutes
Cooking time: 40 minutes
Serves: 2

FINGER LICKIN' PRAWNS

Here is a simple snack of prawns that have been cooked in a little chilli and garlic and served with a dip. The purity of fresh, simply prepared shellfish is just the thing for a moon-lit picnic on the beach.

Ingredients

1 tsp butter

2 tbsp oil

1 garlic clove, finely chopped

1 red chilli, seeds left in
and finely chopped

½ tsp sweet smoked paprika

10 large raw king prawns,
shells on, heads removed

Juice of 1 lemon, plus a few slices
for a finger bowl

Salt and black pepper

½ small bunch parsley,
roughly chopped

For the dip

4 tbsp mayonnaise

1 tbsp tomato ketchup

1 tsp Worcestershire Sauce

A decent dash of Tabasco or
pinch of cayenne pepper

Method

Melt the butter and oil together in a frying pan.

Add the garlic, chilli and paprika and fry for 1 to 2 minutes on a medium heat, then turn up the heat and toss in the prawns.

Fry them for a few minutes, adding the juice of half of the lemon. Keep stirring, until all the prawns turn pink. Take off the heat, season with salt and pepper and pour the remaining half of the lemon juice and the parsley over the top. Let them cool a little and put in the fridge until you need them.

To make the dip, vigorously combine all of the dip ingredients together and decant into a small pot with a lid. Keep it in the fridge until you need it.

Don't forget to take a bottle of water and a bowl for washing your hands – unless you are on the beach, in which case run down to the shoreline and rinse them there. Far more romantic.

Prep time: 5 minutes
Cooking time: 8 minutes
Serves: 2

STICKY CHILLI CHICKEN WINGS

With a decent whack of spiciness, these chicken wings make great finger food. Yes, they are bit messy to eat but surely that's all part of the fun. Make these the day before to allow them to be chilled in the fridge before packing.

Ingredients

12 chicken wings

Oil for cooking

1 lime, cut into wedges for serving

Marinade

Juice of 1 lime, zest of half

75ml sweet chilli sauce, plus extra for dipping

2 tsp soy sauce

1 tbsp ketchup

1 small garlic clove, grated

½ red chilli, deseeded and finely diced

2 tsp olive oil

1 tbsp brown sugar

Sea salt and black pepper

Method

Preheat the oven to 180°C/Fan 160°C/ 350°F/Gas mark 4.

Toss the chicken wings in a little oil to coat them, and season well with salt and pepper. Lay them on a roasting tin and put them in the oven for 25 minutes, turning occasionally.

While they are cooking, mix all of the marinade ingredients together in a large bowl.

Take the wings out of the oven, put them into the bowl and mix well so that they get thoroughly coated with the marinade.

Put a piece of baking parchment on the bottom of the roasting tin. Shake the excess marinade off the chicken (and discard the left-over marinade), lay the chicken pieces in a single layer on the roasting tin and put in to the oven for another 20 minutes. Keep a close eye on them and turn them occasionally. After 20 minutes they should be sticky and crispy on the outside.

Cut into a couple of them to check that the meat is cooked and there are no pink juices running out.

Let them cool thoroughly before packing between layers of baking paper in a sealable storage tub and put in the fridge to chill overnight. Serve with wedges of lime to squeeze over the top and some additional sweet chilli sauce for dipping, as well as plenty of napkins.

Prep time: 10 minutes
Cooking time: 45 minutes
Serves: 2

PEACH, TOMATO & MOZZARELLA SALAD

These flavour combinations work really well, especially if you make sure the tomatoes and peaches are ripe to get the most flavour. It works even better if you use a variety of different sizes and colours of tomato. You can replace the peaches with nectarines and can also swap the basil for mint leaves.

Ingredients

250g ripe, mixed variety tomatoes

2 ripe peaches, or nectarines

1 tbsp balsamic vinegar

3 tbsp olive oil

¼ small red onion, very finely chopped (optional)

100g mozzarella, torn up into small pieces

Around 5 fresh basil leaves

Salt flakes and coarsely ground black pepper

Method

To make this salad, cut the tomatoes and peaches into bite-sized chunks.

Mix the balsamic vinegar and olive oil by putting it in a small, transportable jar with a lid and shaking it.

To serve the salad, combine your peaches and tomatoes with the red onion, if using. Lay the salad on a large wide plate or shallow dish and pop the pieces of mozzarella around the plate between the pieces of tomato and peach. Tear the basil leaves, put on the top and season with salt and pepper.

Drizzle the balsamic vinegar and olive oil dressing across the top, varying the amount according to taste.

I prefer bite-sized chunks as I am more of a rustic girl, but feel free to slice and stack in straight lines if that's more you

Prep time: 10 minutes
Cooking time: none
Serves: 2

SUMMER ROLLS
WITH DIPPING SAUCE

These rolls are summer on a plate – light, fresh and full of flavour, which is why they are so moreish. You will need rice paper wrappers like the ones used for Chinese spring rolls, although these are the unfried version. You can find them in Asian stores, larger supermarkets and online.

Ingredients

12 large prawns, peeled and cooked

Juice of 1 lime

75g dried vermicelli noodles

1 tsp soy sauce

2 radishes, thinly sliced

1 large carrot, peeled and grated thickly

½ red pepper, cut into matchsticks

½ cucumber, deseeded, cut into matchsticks

1 avocado, flesh cut into long, thin slices

2 spring onions, shredded lengthways

2 tbsp roasted cashew or peanuts, roughly chopped

2 sprigs of fresh mint

8 square rice wrap sheets (22cm x 22cm) ➤➤

Method

Put the prawns in a bowl and squeeze the juice of half a lime over them. Put to one side.

Prepare the noodles by putting them in a bowl of boiling water for 4 minutes until softened, but still al dente. Remove, drain and rinse in cold water. Drain again then put the noodles in a bowl and mix with the soy sauce. Put to one side.

Prepare all your vegetables as per the ingredients list. Put them all in piles along the top of your chopping board for easy access as you make the rolls. Put the avocado slices in a dish and squeeze the other half of the lime juice over the top to help stop them going brown.

To make the spring rolls, put an individual rice wrapper in a shallow bowl or on a large dinner plate. Submerge the wrapper in cold water, and jostle it about gently with your fingertips until it softens – just enough to be pliable. If you are a beginner, it might be easier to use two wrappers together as they are less fragile to roll this way.

Keep the wrapper on the plate and pour off all the water, making an effort to really drain it. It will be stuck to the plate so don't worry about it coming off when you shake the plate. Use a sharp knife to cut it in half and put one half to the side. ➤➤

Prep time: 40 minutes
Cooking time: 5 minutes
Makes: 8 rolls

SUMMER ROLLS
WITH DIPPING SAUCE

Dipping sauce

2 tbsp sugar

4 tbsp lime juice

3 tbsp fish sauce

2 garlic cloves, minced
or finely grated

½ small fresh red chilli,
finely sliced

2 tbsp fresh coriander leaves,
finely chopped

Start to arrange your filling on the remaining half. Make the most of the wrappers being see-through by making the layer of filling touching the wrap as highly coloured and artistic as you can. I suggest a line of alternate prawns with circles of radish, framed by cucumber matchsticks. On top of this, add layers of noodles, mixed with nuts and fresh herbs, the carrot, spring onions, red pepper sticks and a slice of avocado through the centre.

Rolling takes a little practise. Bring the top and bottom edges up to just cover the edges of the filling, then bring the left side over the top of the filling and roll the whole thing towards the right. The rice paper is sticky so it should seal itself. To help them stick, lay the rolls seam side down when you store them.

Make the sauce by mixing all the ingredients together in a bowl until the sugar dissolves, or put them all in a lidded jar and shake it vigorously. Decant the sauce into a little dish when you arrive at your picnic.

Try using pork, salmon or even strips of halloumi instead of the prawns, or swap the noodles for rice

MENU IDEAS

1 **Parsnip and squash soup** | **Bread** | **Rich romantic chocolate cake for two**

Simple, for a cosy, wintery snuggle in the sand dunes.

2 **Smoked cheese straws** | **Sticky sweet sesame sausages** | **Summer rolls with dipping sauce** | **Chocolate, orange and pine nut cookies**

Striding out to find your own little corner of the world, this food is easy to carry and good to share.

3 **Smoked salmon and asparagus tartlets** | **Orzo primavera salad** | **Finger lickin' prawns** | **Boozy fruit jellies** | **Strawberry tarts** | **Mango Bellinis**

Pull out all the stops for big love life moments.

4 **Sharing platter** | **Smoked cheese straws** | **Spinach and ricotta boreks** | **Sophisticated shortbread**

First date forays: easy to eat, not too messy, small portions for nervous tummies.

MARVELLOUS PLACES
FOR THE
PERFECT ROMANTIC PICNIC

—— LOCH AN EILEIN ——

ROTHIEMURCHUS, SCOTLAND

Rothiemurchus is a special and beautiful place in the heart of the Cairngorms National Park. The estate owners balance their committed conservation of this native forest with access for the public. Riding and biking trails, watersports centres and even sled-dog rides are on offer. However, there is a place tucked away on this vast highland estate to head to for the most tranquil, romantic setting to place your picnic rug. Loch an Eilein translates from Gaelic as 'Loch of the Island'.

The still waters of Loch an Eilein create a perfect reflection of the surrounding pine trees. At the centre of this loch is a small island, on which sits a ruined 13th-century castle. There are some lovely spots under the trees along the shoreline opposite the island to share your food. It's not a deserted spot, but if you face out to the romantic ruins of this seemingly floating castle, breathe in the smell of pine and watch the red squirrels go about their day, you can still enjoy the romance, peace and tranquillity of this wild place.

FIND IT Loch an Eilein car park is at the end of a minor road to the loch (PH22 1QT is the nearest postcode). There is a charge per person. Take the path from the far end of the car park, signed 'Loch an Eilein'. Follow the path and the occasional signs. It will take about an hour to get to the loch, although the full walk around the loch is a couple of hours.

—— BRONTË FALLS ——

HAWORTH, WEST YORKSHIRE

This is a fabulously wild location to take your date and a basket of food, to walk in the footsteps of Emily Brontë, author of *Wuthering Heights*, one of the greatest love stories of all time. Brontë Falls is actually a tiny waterfall out in the middle of the bleakly beautiful moor, a place where the sisters used to come to sit and write. Instead you can sit with your beau among the patches of purple heather, perhaps read some romance and take in the soul-stirring landscapes of the expansive brooding moorland.

FIND IT Five minutes walk from the village of Haworth (about 10 miles northwest of Bradford) gets you out onto miles of open heather moorland. Find the church in the village and follow the wooden footpath signed to Brontë Falls two and a half miles from there.

THE GREAT STONE OF FOURSTONES

TATHAM FELLS, NORTH YORKSHIRE

Not all romantic picnic spots need to be pretty, fluffy, cosy and secluded. This one is perhaps suited to a post-argument re-set. It's exposed to the elements, it can be raw but it provides a 360-degree view. The breezes will blow away the cobwebs and give you an opportunity to feel on top of the world together.

The Great Stone of Fourstones is an enormous boulder set high up on the moor above the small market town of High Bentham, and rests on the ancient boundary of Yorkshire and Lancashire. The stone has 14 well-worn, stone steps carved into it, so climb them and sit atop with your picnic for a panoramic view of Yorkshire's three peaks: Whernside, Ingleborough and Pen-y-ghent. My suggestion is to pick a good day and head there to watch the sunset over the Lake District in the distance. You'll be serenaded by the ground nesting birds, curlews and lapwings.

It seems odd to find a huge boulder in an otherwise flat landscape. Geologists will tell you it was left here when a glacier melted having carried it from some distant rocky landscape. Presumably at one time there were three others, which have since eroded to nothing. Legend lovers and storytellers have a different view: it was thrown across the Irish Sea by the giant Finn McCool (who built the Giant's Causeway in County Antrim). Make up your own story while you picnic.

FIND IT From High Bentham, head down Station Road and over the river. The road is known as Thickrash Brow. Continue for about a mile and the landscape will open out into the hills. There is a layby on the left-hand side; park here and follow the footpath for about 100 yards. You won't miss it.

PADLEY GORGE

PEAK DISTRICT, DERBYSHIRE

In a deep and narrow valley in the Peak District, you'll find the watery oasis that is Padley Gorge. It's a wooded playground of sun, dappled rockpools and a bubbling stream that meanders among the oaks and silver birches with many places to find picnic spots on the open, grassy banks of the stream.

Further on from the grassy areas, the river tumbles down rocky boulders towards the Derwent Valley below. Head this way if you want some shade and to sit among the tree roots for your snacks, and find a quieter away-from-it-all spot.

FIND IT Park in the Longshaw estate visitor centre car park, just off the A6187 Owler Bar Road. The visitor centre postcode is S11 7TZ.

BEDRUTHAN STEPS BEACH ON A STARRY NIGHT

CORNWALL

Picnics don't have to be during the day. If the forecast is for a clear night, this is a great, atmospheric little Cornish cove in which to have supper under the stars. It has been designated as a Dark Sky Discovery Site, which recognizes excellent places to stargaze due to the low light pollution. It also means that the day-trippers to this popular little beach will have long departed. Make sure you choose to picnic at low tide, though, as the beach can get totally cut off at high tide.

Head down the steep steps from the clifftop and find a spot hidden among the rocky stacks. The stacks all but disappear at high tide, the tops just poking above the water, said to be the stepping stones of the Celtic giant Bedruthan. The 120 steps down to the beach were originally cut into the cliff by smugglers, who stored their bounty in the many caves facing onto this cove.

FIND IT Park in the National Trust car park at TR8 4BU. It is just off B3276 from Newquay to Padstow, 6 miles southwest of Padstow.

A PICNIC BY THE PATH

MEWSLADE BAY & FALL BAY, GOWER PENINSULA

The walk from Rhossili, around Worm's Head and along the rugged coastline, via the Pembrokeshire coastal path, is a real soul stirrer. You'll get spectacular gulls'-eye views of two of the prettiest bays in this part of Wales. In fact, some people believe that Mewslade Bay got its name from the old word 'Mew', meaning seagull, possibly because the limestone cliffs surrounding it are home to colonies of seabirds. You can reach both beaches from the path if you want a picnic on the sand. However, be aware that they completely disappear at high tide. My particular favourite picnic spot along here is a large, horizontal limestone slab of a rock that serves perfectly as a table for two. Table with a sea view anyone?

FIND IT Park in Rhossili and start heading towards Worm's Head (you can't miss it). Follow the walking track along by the wall and past the old coastguard hut that is now used as a visitor centre, turn left and follow the cliff path – this is the one that will take you past the two bays. You can either come back the way you came, or do a loop via the village of Pitton if you want a good walk.

—— LLANDDWYN ISLAND ——

ANGLESEY

Llanddwyn Island (Ynys Llanddwyn) is a magical place. Find it at the far end of the beach near Newborough Warren, a raw and beautifully wild habitat of marram grass sand dunes and trails through woodland. The island is in fact a narrow finger of land, attached to the mainland other than at the highest tide. It is perfect for a remote 'away from the world' picnic. Even more appropriate is that it was named after Dwynwen, a fifth-century princess and the Welsh patron saint of lovers. There are lovely views of Snowdonia, and some great options for exploring among the rocks to watch the wildlife. The whole place is impossibly romantic, but if you really want an unforgettable picnic moment choose sunrise or sunset. It's proposal material.

FIND IT Cross the Menai Strait via the A55. Take the A5 and then follow the A4080 west to reach Newborough. Once in Newborough, turn left down Church Street signposted Llys Rhosyr (opposite the post office). In 2 miles, this road leads you through Newborough Forest to the extensive parking area at Llanddwyn Beach.

—— GRANCHESTER MEADOWS ——

CAMBRIDGE

Granchester Meadows are beautiful meadows next to the River Cam, just to the south of Cambridge. The meadows are loved by locals as a place to find some peace and quiet out of the city.

It's a pretty place for a walk and a talk before settling down to dine by the river. This is a good one for a first date perhaps. You won't be on your own, as it is one of the city's most famous green spaces, but there will be plenty of things to watch and comment on. Keep an eye out for the kingfishers and herons, and the people floating slowly by in their punts pirouetting with the wild swimmers. There are always dog walkers and buggy strollers – it's a veritable highway of meadow meanderers. The footpath along the river takes you to the picturesque village of Granchester so just choose a suitable spot along the way.

FIND IT Park in Lammas Land car park and the meadows can be reached from here.

—— FAIRY POOLS ——

ISLE OF SKYE, SCOTLAND

Pretty much anywhere on the Isle of Skye can make you feel romantic. The scenery envelops you with its beauty. But there is one particular spot to take your loved one to that is unforgettable for its loveliness. Fairy Pools, at the foot of the Back Cuillin mountains, is a worthy spot for a proposal. It's a series of crystal blue rock pools and fairy-sized waterfalls. If you are alone, take a dip in the pool. And that's the key – you need to be alone to make this picnic spot purely magical, so visit early in the morning for a breakfast picnic or a sunset supper to truly cast the spell. It's a hearty 40-minute walk, but thoroughly worth it.

FIND IT The nearest village to the Fairy Pools is Carbost in the west of Skye. Park in the Forestry Commision gravel car park signposted 'Glumagan Na Sithichean' and Fairy Pools (nearest postcode is IV47 8TA). It is located along the single track road that leads to Glenbrittle from Carbost. Follow the signposted walking track to the pools.

—— ST DUNSTAN'S CHURCH RUIN ——

LONDON EC3

The words romantic and ruin seem to come as a pair. Luckily, Britain is strewn with a bounty of ivy-encrusted manor houses, tumbling towers and crag-top castles just dripping with atmosphere for lovers to feast among the follies and relics.

St Dunstan's is a hidden gem, tucked down an alleyway close to the Tower of London. This is the crumbled ruin of an 11th-century church that has been through a lot: damaged in the Great Fire of London, later repaired and given a new steeple by Sir Christopher Wren, then bombed in the war. It was decided not to rebuild it.

It wasn't until 1967 that the City of London decided to plant it with gardens to provide a public green space. It is now a haven away from city life, a quiet space filled with shrubs, and trees, making St Dunstan's an impossibly romantic setting for a picnic for two.

FIND IT St Dunstan's Hill, London, EC3R 5DD. The nearest tube is Monument or Tower Hill.

3

COOL BOXES

FOR GATHERINGS, GROUPS AND FEASTS WITH FRIENDS

Every summer my family, Nan, 12 uncles, aunties and 16 cousins went to the New Forest together for the day. We went to play cricket and have a picnic as no pub or restaurant could seat us for lunch. Good job really. A picnic was the ideal feast for the occasion. All of my aunts bought Tupperware full of quiche and peeled boiled eggs, and the kids ate Monster Munch. It was brilliant. Everyone was relaxed, there was no fuss about having to behave at a table and we ate what we wanted, when we wanted – between overs.

I still believe that feasting in a group is both one of life's greatest pleasures and privileges. The chatter, the company and the sense of belonging is life affirming. Food is the perfect excuse to bring people together.

Post-party brunches on the beach, a big 'O' party picnic or even trays of food for open days and fêtes, catering for these groups needs to be mostly easy, not too expensive and with a few impressive centrepiece dishes thrown in for good measure. For this I've included a glazed ham and baked side of salmon, as for the rest, pile it high with stylish salads and traybakes for pud.

All the recipes in this chapter have been designed to feed 12. Just double up or halve the volumes where needed.

GIN-BAKED SALMON

I know the traditional way to prepare a centrepiece salmon is to poach it, but I prefer to bake mine to add a bit of colour, which looks more appetizing. Baking doesn't have to mean the fish is drier – by adding a little gin to the baking tray, it creates a beautifully flavoured steam that produces a perfectly moist fish.

Ingredients

1.5kg side of salmon, filleted

3 large lemons, cut into thin slices, plus 1 heaped tsp unwaxed lemon zest

4 large garlic cloves, skins on

3 tbsp olive oil

100ml gin (or use white wine)

Salt and black pepper

3 tbsp honey

3 tbsp soy sauce

A small sprig of dill

Method

Preheat the oven to 200°C/Fan 180°C/400°F/Gas mark 6.

Line a large roasting tin with foil, large enough so that it comes up the sides a little. Add a piece of baking parchment on top of the foil. Lay the lemon slices and garlic all across the bottom of the tin and lay the salmon fillet on top. You may have to cut the salmon side in half to fit it in your tin, or use two roasting tins, but you can easily put it back together to serve it and hide the cut with some lemon slices. If using two roasting tins, use an extra 100ml of gin to create enough steam in the second tin.

Drizzle the oil over the salmon and season with salt and pepper. Whisk together the honey and soy sauce, and brush or pour half of this all over the fish. Sprinkle the lemon zest over the top and pour the gin around the fish.

Seal the tin with another piece of foil to make a lid and bake in the oven for 15 minutes. Then take off the foil, pour the rest of the honey and soy mix over the fish and cook without the foil for another 15 minutes.

Remove from the oven and let it cool for about 10 minutes.

Carefully lift the fish out of the roasting tin by using the edges of the foil and lower it into the container you are going to transport it in. Pour any cooking juices over the top and allow it all to cool in the box in the fridge. Serve with homemade tartare sauce (see page 246), wedges of lemon and a little fresh dill across the top.

Prep time: 15 minutes
Cooking time: 30 minutes
Serves: 12

FIERY NUT
& NOODLE SALAD

Feeding groups can be costly. This incredibly moreish recipe is high on favour and relatively low on cost. Put the effort into chopping all your veggies and the rest is a case of mixing and assembling. I've used one chilli but use more if you prefer a hot kick. If you don't have coconut milk, the dressing works well without, giving it a more fiery, zesty finish.

Ingredients

350g dried medium egg noodles

1 tbsp sesame oil

12 spring onions

5 large carrots, peeled

2 large cucumbers, deseeded

4 red peppers, deseeded

1 small red chilli, deseeded

300g unsalted roasted peanuts

2 tins water chestnuts (optional)

1 bunch of fresh coriander

For the dressing

3 tbsp sweet chilli sauce

5 tbsp crunchy peanut butter

4 tbsp coconut milk

1 tbsp honey

Juice of 2 large limes

5 tbsp light soy sauce

2 tbsp rice or white wine vinegar

2 large garlic cloves, minced

3cm piece of fresh ginger, grated

Method

Cook the noodles according to instructions – don't overcook them as they need to retain some bite. As soon as they are cooked, drain them and rinse with cold water. Let them drain some more and then put them into the tub you are going to take the salad in and toss them in the sesame oil. Put to one side while you prepare the vegetables.

Cut the roots off the spring onions and thinly slice them on the diagonal, including the green bits. Cut the carrots, cucumbers and red peppers into thin matchsticks (no thicker than 1cm). Finely slice the chilli.

Toss the chopped vegetables in with the noodles. Roughly chop the peanuts, drain and thinly slice the water chestnuts (if using) and mix these in.

Make the dressing by whisking together all of the ingredients with a seasoning of salt and pepper until it is well combined.

Pour the dressing, as much or as little as you like, over the noodles and vegetables and mix well. Serve with chopped coriander leaves on the top.

Try adding shredded chicken, prawns or marinated tofu pieces

Prep time: 20 minutes
Cooking time: 10 minutes
Serves: 12 as a side

ORANGE ZEST BROWNIES

Everyone loves a brownie. These have a double chocolate hit from the cocoa and the chocolate chips, and are given an orange twist with the orange juice. You could use chopped-up orange-flavoured chocolate instead of the chocolate chips. If it's grown-ups only, then add a couple of tablespoons of orange liqueur to the mix.

Ingredients

230g salted butter

400g caster sugar

1 tsp vanilla extract

½ tsp salt

65g cocoa powder

4 medium eggs

220g self-raising flour, sieved

100g chocolate chips

Zest of 1 large orange, juice of half of it

30.5cm x 18cm baking tray

Method

Preheat the oven to 180°C/Fan 160°C/350°F/Gas mark 4.

Line the tray with baking parchment. You can make this in a foil baking tray, lined with baking parchment, which means you can take the tray with you to the picnic.

Melt the butter and pour into a large bowl. Add the sugar, vanilla extract, salt and cocoa powder and mix well.

Add the eggs one at a time, and beat them in. Add a tablespoon of flour with each egg.

Sift in the rest of the flour a bit a time and mix thoroughly. Finally stir through the chocolate chips.

Once all mixed, pour into the tray and use the back of a spoon to push it into the corners.

Bake in the centre of the oven for 25 minutes. When they are done they should be crisp on top and soft in the middle. As soon as you take it out of the oven, squeeze the juice of half an orange all over the top, then sprinkle on the zest of the whole orange.

Allow them to cool, then cut into 12 generous portions or 24 bite-sized ones. If you want to save time

Prep time: 20 minutes
Cooking time: 25 minutes
Makes: 24 bite-sized pieces

POTATO SALAD

For this simple dish, there is one detail that you need to get right. Use a waxy potato, not a floury one that will fall apart when you mix it in the dressing. Next, to mayo or not to mayo? Or just some oil, salt and herbs? They all have their merits – this version is light, simple and delicious and uses yoghurt instead of mayonnaise.

Ingredients

1.4kg Jersey Royals or Charlotte potatoes

3 garlic cloves, skin on

8 radishes

8 spring onions

Dressing

6 tbsp natural yoghurt

6 tbsp crème fraîche

1 tbsp horseradish sauce

2 tsp lemon juice

2 tsp caster sugar

Salt and black pepper

Method

Put the potatoes and garlic cloves in a large pan of salted, boiling water and boil them for 10 minutes until they are tender. Drain them and discard the garlic. When the potatoes are cool enough to handle, cut them in half, or quarters depending on their size.

Thinly slice the radishes into rounds; thinly slice the spring onions too.

Make the dressing by combining all of the dressing ingredients in a large bowl and whisking well to combine it.

Add the cool potatoes, radishes and spring onions and mix gently.

Try replacing the radishes and horseradish with handfuls of chopped fresh mint, coriander and parsley

Prep time: 10 minutes
Cooking time: 10 minutes
Serves: 12 as a side

MEXICAN BEAN & PEPPER SALAD

Bean salads are silly easy to make, yet impressive to eat. It's just an added bonus that they also happen to be really healthy, so you can eat extra dessert and still feel pretty virtuous. This one sings out with all the punch of harissa and fresh lime in its Mexican-style dressing.

Ingredients

400g tin black beans

400g tin aduki or kidney beans

400g tin sweetcorn

1 green pepper, deseeded

1 yellow pepper, deseeded

½ mild green chilli, deseeded and finely chopped

2 tbsp chives, chopped

Salt and black pepper

2 tbsp coriander, chopped

2 handfuls (approx 50 grams) of plain tortilla chips, lightly crushed

Dressing

1 tsp harissa

½ tsp smoked paprika

½ tsp ground cumin

Salt and black pepper

Juice of 1 lime

½ tbsp sherry or red wine vinegar

2 tbsp olive oil

Method

Rinse and drain all the tinned beans and sweetcorn, then put them in a sealable container that you will transport and serve the salad in.

Dice the peppers and add to the beans, along with the chilli and chives, and season with salt and pepper.

In a small bowl or jar with a lid, whisk or shake together all of the dressing ingredients before combining with the bean salad.

The tortilla chips and coriander are best added just before serving, so take them in a separate freezer bag or just place them across the top of the salad before leaving for the picnic and mix them into the beans before serving.

Prep time: 20 minutes
Cooking time: none
Serves: 12 as a side

LEMON & GINGER CHEESECAKE BITES

A popular pudding made as a picnic traybake. Aside from melting some butter, there is no cooking involved – just plenty of chilling. These delicious little bite-sized cheesecakes are light and summery with a punch of citrusy flavours. You can play around with it by leaving out the lemon and blueberries and adding a topping of freshly sliced mango.

Ingredients

300g crushed ginger biscuits

150g unsalted butter

500g mascarpone cheese

140g caster sugar

Juice and zest of 1 large unwaxed lemon

Juice and zest of 1 small lime

2 handfuls of blueberries

5 or 6 mint leaves

30.5cm x 18cm baking tray

Method

Line the baking tray with baking parchment.

Melt the butter in a saucepan, add the crushed ginger biscuits and give it a good mix.

Press the mixture evenly and firmly into the tray, then put in the freezer for an hour.

Mix the mascarpone, caster sugar, juice of the whole lemon along with half the lemon zest, juice of the whole lime and half the lime zest. Once all ingredients are combined, pour the mixture over the biscuit base.

Sprinkle the blueberries and chopped mint leaves over the top of the cheesecake. Put the rest of the lemon and lime zest over the cheesecake and refrigerate for at least 3 hours before cutting into 24 bite-sized pieces.

This tastes best if made the day before

Prep time: 15 minutes
Cooking time: 3 to 4 hours to chill
Makes: 24 bite-sized pieces

MY MUM'S PICNIC PIE

A traditional-looking pie like this one shouts 'PICNIC' like no other. My mum makes this for every big family weekend gathering and it is always one of the first things to get gobbled up. Here I'm using shop-bought pastry, but if you want to go the whole hog, make the pastry on page 247.

Ingredients

700g sausage meat

400g shop-bought shortcrust pastry

4 hard boiled eggs, peeled and sliced

4 large tomatoes, sliced

1 tbsp Dijon mustard

1 additional egg, to egg wash the pastry

23cm fluted, loose-bottom flan tin, well-greased

Method

Preheat the oven to 180°C/Fan 160°C/350°F/Gas mark 4.

Divide the pastry into two pieces, one slightly larger than the other. Roll them out and use the larger piece to line the flan tin, pushing the sides into the fluted edges.

Divide the sausage meat into three equal pieces. Cover a chopping board with cling film, place the sausage meat on the top then cover with another piece of cling film. Roll each piece out into a circle to fit the flan tin. Rolling it this way stops the sausage meat sticking to the rolling pin.

Place the first circle of sausage meat onto the pastry in the tin, then arrange slices of egg to cover it in a single layer. Place the second circle of sausage meat on top of the egg, spread the mustard across it and arrange the slices of tomato to cover the sausage meat. Finally add the third circle of sausage meat.

Cover with the smaller pastry circle and seal the edges of the pie by brushing them with a little water and 'crimping' them to seal. Cut three slits in the middle of the pastry top (about 3cm long and 1cm apart) to let the steam out as it cooks. Brush the surface with the beaten egg. Place the flan tin on a metal baking sheet.

Bake in the oven for 15 minutes then turn the heat down to 160°C/Fan 140°C/325°F/Gas mark 3 and bake for another 1 hour and 30 minutes. Allow to cool before refrigerating. Serve on a wooden board, cut into 12 wedges.

Prep time: 35 minutes
Cooking time: 1 hour 45 mins
Serves: 12

CORONATION
CHICKEN SALAD

Rather than make the curry dressing from scratch, I use a good-quality curry paste. It saves time, which matters when you are making a picnic for a crowd. My advice is to transport the different elements of this salad in separate tubs and assemble it in situ.

Ingredients

8 large chicken breasts

2 tbsp rapeseed or ground nut oil

100ml hot chicken stock

150g sultanas

200g natural yoghurt

100g mayonnaise

6 tbsp mango chutney

4 tbsp korma paste

1 large bunch of fresh coriander

2 red onions, diced

300g watercress

3 ripe mangoes, peeled and cut into cubes

50g flaked almonds, toasted

Juice of 1 lime

Method

Preheat the oven to 180°C/Fan 160°C/350°F/Gas mark 4.

Heat the oil in a large frying pan and fry the chicken breasts until they are golden on each side. You may have to do this in batches.

Next, put the chicken breasts into a large roasting tin, pour in the hot chicken stock around them, cover the tin with foil and seal it around the edges. Place in the oven and cook for about 18 minutes. Then take out of the oven and allow the chicken to cool in the liquid for 10 minutes – no more. Cut into a chicken breast to check it is cooked through.

Use a sharp knife to cut all of the chicken breasts into neat slices. Cover the chicken and put to one side.

Put the sultanas in a bowl and cover them in hot water – this will plump them up and make them juicier.

In a bowl combine the yoghurt, mayonnaise, mango chutney, korma paste and half the coriander leaves. Add the diced red onion, the sliced chicken and the sultanas and gently mix to coat.

When ready to serve, arrange the watercress across a large wooden board or large shallow serving bowl. Scatter the mango cubes across it, then spoon the chicken mixture across the top, and sprinkle over the remaining coriander leaves.

Finally, scatter the toasted almond flakes over the top and a squeeze of lime juice.

Prep time: 10 minutes
Cooking time: 30 minutes
Serves: 12 as a side

ORANGE &
FIVE SPICE COLESLAW

A simple addition of Chinese five spice transforms a standard coleslaw into something really special. The fresh orange pieces give it a wonderful summery lift too. This is great served with the tropical picnic ham.

Ingredients

3 large carrots, grated

12 spring onions, sliced on a slant

½ white cabbage, sliced and shredded

½ red cabbage, sliced and shredded

250g celeriac, peeled and grated

1 cucumber, cut into thin lengths

½ small red onion, peeled and diced finely

3 oranges

6 tbsp mayonnaise

100ml crème fraîche

1 heaped tsp sugar

2 tsp Chinese five spice

Juice of ½ lime

3 tbsp pumpkin seeds (optional)

Salt and black pepper

Method

Put all the cut, sliced and shredded vegetables into a bowl.

Peel two of the oranges and roughly cut into small pieces, then add to the vegetables.

In a separate bowl put the mayonnaise, crème fraîche, sugar, two large pinches of salt, five spice, lime juice and juice of half an orange.

Mix vigorously with a fork. It will look a bit lumpy at first but have faith and keep mixing – it should end up as quite a thin-looking dressing. Add in the pumpkin seeds, if using.

Toss the dressing thoroughly through the vegetables. If you prefer a more unctuous consistency, add another tablespoon of crème fraîche.

Grate a little orange zest over the top, season with salt and pepper and mix.

You can decorate the top with slices of the remaining orange before serving.

Prep time: 20 minutes
Cooking time: none
Serves: 12 as a side

PEAR & BLUE CHEESE TART

As impressive to look at as it is to eat, this is an easy, assembly-type recipe that uses legendary flavour combinations. Sometimes it's best not to mess with a classic.

Ingredients

4 firm pears

15g unsalted butter

2 tbsp balsamic vinegar

A handful of walnut or pecan halves

375g pre-rolled puff pastry

150g blue cheese, such as perl las blue or stilton

A large handful of watercress leaves

Salt and black pepper

Method

Preheat the oven to 200°C/Fan 180°C/400°F/Gas mark 6.

Core and cut the pears into wedges, about eight for each pear.

Melt the butter with the balsamic vinegar in a large frying pan, then add the pear wedges and the nuts, and fry them until the pears begin to colour and caramelise a little. This should take about 3 to 4 minutes. Remove from the heat and put to one side.

Lay the sheet of pastry flat on a piece of baking parchment. Score a border about 2cm from the edges.

Keeping it on the baking parchment, transfer to a baking tray. Don't forget to do this first – otherwise you'll struggle to lift a loaded piece of pastry across to your tray.

Arrange the pear pieces, the crumbled blue cheese and the nuts across the pastry. Give it all a good seasoning with salt and pepper.

Bake for 20 minutes in the oven until the pastry is golden and puffed up around the edges.

Pack the tart for transportation, then just before serving scatter the watercress over it and cut into 12 pieces.

Prep time: 20 minutes
Cooking time: 20 minutes
Serves: 12 as a side

PINEAPPLE SALSA WITH FRESH MINT

The fusion of fresh flavours makes this salsa a fabulous complement to either the salmon or the tropical picnic ham recipes. The mint and the chilli add a great cool-versus-spice play off on your tongue.

Ingredients

2 medium-sized ripe pineapples, cored and peeled

2 red peppers, deseeded

2 small red onion, peeled

400g sweetcorn
(from a tin is fine)

Juice and zest of 1 large lime

½ red chilli, finely chopped

1 heaped tsp caster sugar

2 large pinches of salt

12 large fresh mint leaves

Method

Chop the pineapple, pepper and onion into equally sized small pieces of about 1cm and put into a bowl that you can transport to your picnic.

Add the sweetcorn, the lime juice, zest, chopped chilli, sugar and salt, and mix together. Finally chop the mint leaves and stir them into the mix.

Put in the fridge to chill until ready to take to the picnic.

Prep time: 10 minutes
Cooking time: none
Serves: 12 as a side

TOMATO, ASPARAGUS & SAUSAGE PASTA

Here's my curiously delicious pasta for a hungry crowd. I don't think I'm alone in loving a cold sausage – so I've oomphed up a pasta salad by adding some fabulous mini fennel meatballs. I promise that the saltiness from the anchovies combines beautifully with the sweet roasted tomatoes and savoury sausage meat to make an addictive bowl of pasta.

Ingredients

Around 40 cherry tomatoes, cut in half

2 tins anchovies, drained and chopped into 1cm pieces

Olive oil

30 spears of asparagus, woody ends cut off and spears cut into 4cm lengths

750g farfalle pasta

Pack of 8 good-quality, thick pork sausages (about 600g)

1 heaped tsp fennel seeds

2 garlic cloves, minced

3 tbsp balsamic vinegar

Juice of ½ lemon

200g parmesan, finely grated

Salt and black pepper

A large handful of fresh basil, roughly chopped

Method

Preheat the oven to 190°C/Fan 170°C/375°F/Gas mark 5.

Line a roasting tray with baking parchment and lay the tomato halves, cut side up, on the tray. Drizzle them with a little olive oil. Dot the anchovy pieces across the tops of the tomatoes and put into the oven to roast for 20 minutes.

Meanwhile, bring a large pan of water to the boil, add a couple of decent pinches of salt and cook the pasta according to the instructions. Add the asparagus after 10 minutes.

Drain the pasta and asparagus, refresh under cold water, drain again, then drizzle a little olive oil over them and fork it through.

Slit the skins of the sausages and push out the sausage meat. Heat two teaspoons of oil in a large frying pan and tip the sausage meat into it. Add the fennel seeds and the garlic cloves. Fry the meat and break it up as it cooks, season with salt and pepper, and add the vinegar after a couple of minutes. When the meat has cooked and has started to get lovely caramelised edges, tip the meat, oils and seeds into the cooked pasta.

When the tomatoes have roasted, add them to the pasta, tipping in any juices as well. Squeeze the lemon juice in and stir. Season again with salt and pepper and add half of the parmesan.

Decant the pasta into a sealable container and store in the fridge. On the day of your picnic, take the basil and the rest of the grated parmesan to mix through the salad when you serve it.

Prep time: 10 minutes
Cooking time: 30 minutes
Serves: 12

JAR OF PICKLED CUCUMBERS

I grew up in South Africa so we ate outside a lot and my Auntie Estelle would always bring a selection of her homemade pickles. This is based on her Jar of Pickled Cucumbers. She used to replace some of the vinegar with water to make it more kid-friendly but these days I can handle the full astringent whack. Adjust to your (and your kids') tastes.

Ingredients

1 large or 2 small cucumbers

1 red onion

2 garlic cloves

1 tbsp white mustard seeds

250ml cider vinegar

250ml white wine vinegar

150g light brown sugar

1 tsp salt

1 tsp black peppercorns

1 small red chilli

A 500ml jar (ideally a sealable Kilner-style jar)

Method

Ideally keep this in the fridge for two days before serving.

Prepare your vegetables. Cut the cucumbers in half lengthways and then into thick slices – about 0.5cm thick. Cut the red onion in half, then into thin slices and put in a bowl of cold water. Thinly slice the peeled garlic cloves.

Put the mustard seeds into a dry frying pan and heat them for a couple of minutes to release the flavour. Use a spatula to keep them moving so that they don't burn.

Put the vinegars, salt, peppercorns, sugar and mustard seeds into a large saucepan and heat gently until the sugar dissolves. Take off the heat and allow the mixture to cool.

Drain the onion and put it into a clean preserving jar along with the cucumber, garlic and chilli and pour over the cooled liquid to cover it.

Seal the jar and leave the pickles in the fridge for 48 hours before eating. It's worth the wait, especially if served alongside the tropical picnic ham.

Prep time: 15 minutes
Cooking time: 10 minutes
Makes: 500ml jar

SPINACH & RICOTTA
BOREK

I had my first taste of borek on holiday in Croatia. The flavours are soft and subtle, and there's something wonderful about the light, crunchy exterior around a creamy delicate filling that makes these so lovely. For this recipe I've changed it about a bit: I've made them into cigar shapes for easy eating and used ricotta instead of feta, although both are good.

Ingredients

50g unsalted butter

3 red onions, finely diced

3 garlic cloves, minced

375g spinach

1 tsp unwaxed lemon zest

3 tsp lemon juice

½ tsp flaked sea salt

¼ tsp nutmeg

½ tsp coarsely ground black pepper

300g ricotta cheese or crumbled feta (or a mix of both)

12 sheets of filo pastry

Olive oil

Method

Preheat the oven to 200°C/Fan 180°C/400°F/Gas mark 6.

Gently melt the butter in a frying pan, add the onions and garlic and cook on a low heat for about 10 minutes until the onions are really soft.

Meanwhile, put the spinach in a large bowl and pour boiling water over the top. Push it down into the water so it's all covered and leave for about 5 minutes in order to let it wilt. Drain and rinse with cold water. Using your hands, gather up the wilted spinach and squeeze out all the excess water.

You'll end up with a green ball. Use a sharp knife to chop it up into smaller pieces. Add this into the frying pan, mix and heat with the onion and garlic for the final couple of minutes of cooking.

Tip the mixture into a bowl and add the lemon zest, lemon juice, nutmeg, salt, pepper and cheese. Mix it all together thoroughly.

Lay three pieces of filo pastry on top of each other and cut into four triangles by cutting diagonally from top left corner to the bottom right corner and vice versa. Spread two tablespoons of the cheese mixture in the middle of the pastry in a line, but close to the long side of the triangle. Fold the sides in and then start to roll the pastry to make a cigar shape.

Brush the cigars over with some olive oil and put on greaseproof paper on a baking tray. Bake in the oven for 20 minutes until they are crunchy and golden. Leave them to cool before packing.

Prep time: 10 minutes
Cooking time: 30 minutes
Makes: 12

PICNIC
PISSALADIERE

Another favourite of mine. This looks fabulous and tastes divine – the saltiness of the olives and anchovies play deliciously against the sweetness of the slow-cooked onions and the thin layer of rich, sweet tomato sauce. A true pissaladiere doesn't have the tomato base, but I think it's a lovely addition.

Ingredients

3 large onions

50g butter

150ml passata

1 tbsp sweet wine or sherry (optional)

1 tsp light brown sugar

2 garlic cloves, crushed

1 heaped tsp thyme, fresh or dried

Salt and black pepper

375g pre-rolled puff pastry

2 tins anchovies

Around 15 black olives, destoned

Method

Preheat the oven to 200°C/Fan 180°C/400°F/Gas mark 6.

Peel and slice the onions and cook them on a low heat in the butter until they are beautifully soft, translucent and incredibly sweet. It will take a good 15 to 20 minutes to achieve the perfect pissaladiere onion.

While they are cooking, make the sauce. Put the passata, sweet wine (if using), sugar, garlic cloves, thyme and a good seasoning of salt and pepper into a saucepan and cook it low and slow – also for about 20 minutes – until it reduces and thickens.

Let it cool a little then use a hand blender to make it smooth.

Roll the pastry out and place on baking parchment, then on a baking tray. Score around it about 1cm from the edge. Thinly spread the sauce across the pastry. Then spread the onions evenly across it too, making sure it is fully covered.

Next, lay the anchovies so that they make diamond criss-crosses across the pastry and finally pop a black olive in the middle of each diamond.

Put in the oven for 20 minutes.

When it is cooked and the pastry has puffed up, slide the tart onto a rack to cool, then cut into 12 squares and pack it up for your picnic.

Prep time: 15 minutes
Cooking time: 40 minutes
Serves: 12

TROPICAL PICNIC HAM

This great looking (and tasting) ham is an ideal centrepiece for a group picnic. It's been cooked in tropical juice and given a fruity glaze to finish. Serve it with the pineapple salsa and the orange and Chinese five spice coleslaw and you'll have yourself an exotic and fruity little picnic spread.

Ingredients

2.2kg smoked boned gammon joint

750ml apple-based tropical fruit juice (such as a blend of apple, orange, mango and pineapple)

2 star anise

125g soft brown sugar

1 heaped tsp fennel seeds

Large stock pot with a lid

Method

As gammon joints are quite salty, it's worth trying to remove a little of the excess salt, so put the joint into a large stock pot and fill with water. Bring to the boil for 15 minutes, then take the gammon out and discard the water.

Give the pan a rinse to remove anything left in the pot. Put the gammon back in and pour in 500ml of fruit juice, then top the rest of the pan up with water until it just covers the ham. Pop the star anise in and once again bring the pan to the boil.

This time when it reaches boiling point, turn the heat down and let it simmer gently with the lid on for about an hour and a half.

Turn the heat off and let the ham sit in its stock for about 20 minutes, then take it out to allow it cool a little.

Preheat the oven to 200°C/Fan 180°C/400°F/Gas mark 6.

To make the glaze, put the remaining 250ml of juice into a saucepan with the brown sugar and the fennel seeds. Bring it up to the boil, stirring continuously to prevent the sugar burning.

Let it bubble away for about 10 minutes, or until the volume of liquid has reduced and it is beginning to thicken. ➤➤

Prep time: 20 minutes
Cooking time: 2 hours 15 minutes
Serves: 12

TROPICAL
PICNIC HAM

➤→ When the joint is cool enough to handle, use a sharp knife to take off the skin and some of the fat, making sure that you leave about 1cm of fat. Make criss-cross diamond shapes in the remaining fat by scoring it diagonally.

Line a roasting tin with foil and place the joint on top. Brush the sticky glaze all over the fat of the ham and put it in the oven for 25 minutes, basting it half way through.

When the joint is done, it will have some lovely crunchy brown, sticky parts to the criss-cross fat pattern. If it hasn't browned, leave it in the oven for a little longer.

Let it cool enough to wrap it in greaseproof paper and put in the fridge until ready to pack it for your picnic. Don't forget to take a wooden board to serve it on and a sharp knife to slice it with.

MENU IDEAS

1 **Pissaladiere** | **Feta, courgette, pea and mint frittata** | **Mexican bean and pepper salad** | **Super smoothies**

The Morning-After-The-Night-Before Brunch. These dishes are quick to make with comforting carbs, energy from eggs and beans plus reviving smoothies.

2 **Gin-baked salmon** | **Tomato, asparagus and sausage pasta** | **Coronation chicken salad** | **Fiery nut and noodle salad** | **Elderflower and raspberry Victoria sponge**

For cricket in the park: a salmon centrepiece and stylish salads for a genteel spread between wickets.

3 **Picnic pie** | **Pear and blue cheese tart** | **Spinach and ricotta boreks** | **Lemon and ginger cheesecake bites** | **Orange zest brownies** | **Fruit**

A picnic for a beach gathering – dishes that don't need a plate.

4 **Tropical picnic ham** | **Pissaladiere** | **New potato and broad bean salad** | **Sticky sweet sesame sausages** | **Pineapple salsa** | **Orange and five spice coleslaw** | **Jewelled cous cous salad** | **Red, white and green pasta salad** | **Pizza puff spirals** | **Cinnamon butter popcorn** | **Strawberry rocky roads** | **Banana and blueberry loaf cake**

A big list for a big birthday celebration. Pile-it-high catering for friends and family of all ages.

MARVELLOUS PLACES
FOR THE
PERFECT
GROUP
PICNIC

—— HEAVEN'S GATE ——

LONGLEAT, WILTSHIRE

And it is heavenly. A walk through pretty woodland opens out on to this elevated grassy spot with views over the grand Longleat estate and the surrounding Wiltshire countryside. It's a truly magical spot to watch the sunset, as well as having an elevated view of the annual Hot Air Balloon Fiesta that takes place on the estate. There is plenty of space to run, play frisbee, build dens in the woods and explore the pair of vast stone sculptures. My top tip is to seek out what must be one of the most perfectly placed rope swings in the country. It swings out over the edge of the hill with the views of Longleat in front of you. To find it, head down through the trees to the left from the grassy area.

FIND IT The free car park is at Nockatts Coppice (nearest postcode is BA12 7PU). There are plenty of parking spaces. Cross the road to pick up the path that winds for about half a mile through a beautifully maintained stretch of rhododendrons, shrubs and varied trees. Head on through thicker woodland to a sturdy gate, which opens out to the heavenly view – hence the name.

—— CADBURY CASTLE ——

SOMERSET

Still called Cadbury Castle despite never having been an actual castle, this is an amazing spot to take a group for a picnic and a run around. It is the largest hill fort in Somerset, rising up from verdant pastures. With Glastonbury Tor visible in the distance, the whole area is steeped in myth and legend. Cadbury Castle is renowned as (one of the many possible sites of) Arthur's Camelot. You can walk the 360-degree trail around the top of what would have been the ramparts and look down on the stillness of the surrounding pastures, farms and cottages. The wide-reaching views are truly spectacular.

Either set up your picnic on the ridge with the views, or take over a space in the hollowed centre for your gathering. There is a woodland down one side for children to explore and run off the feast.

FIND IT South Cadbury is off the A303. There is a free car park in the village at the bottom of the hill. Go past the church and around the corner. You will see the car park sign posted on the left. To reach the picnic spot, walk out of the car park, turn right. When you reach the first house, you'll see a stony track on your left that leads up to Cadbury Castle. It will take about 10 minutes from the car park.

SPITCHWICK COMMON

NEWBRIDGE, DARTMOOR

There is plentiful drama in Dartmoor's landscapes to please every type of picnicker: remote moorland, rivers and tops of tors with far reaching views of the sea. This particular spot, Spitchwick Common, is a wonderful meeting point for groups. On the banks of the beautiful River Dart, Spitchwick has a grassy area that is perfect (and popular) for picnics, games of boules and cricket. It is also a top spot for swimming in the river. There are deep and shallow spots to suit your courage and a footpath that runs alongside the river for a post-picnic stroll too.

FIND IT There is parking at Newbridge (nearest postcode is TQ13 7NT). Take the road from Ashburton signposted towards Newbridge. You'll drive across the narrow New Bridge over the Dart and you'll see the car park. Follow the north bank of the river under the bridge to Spitchwick. The grassy area will be in front of you.

WINTERTON BEACH

NORFOLK

Norfolk has an array of picnic-perfect beaches to choose from. The wide sandy beaches means you'll never feel hemmed in, even in the height of summer. One hidden gem is Winterton beach. An unspoilt stretch of the softest white sand is backed by the Winterton Dunes Nature Reserve and woodland. It can be accessed via the pretty fishing village of Winterton-on-Sea. The beach is so wide that is doesn't matter whether the tide is in or out, there's plenty of dry sand to park your party.

The Horsey end of the beach is home to a colony of grey seals. During the winter months, the seals come ashore to give birth and you can see the pups on the beach with their mothers, but please keep your distance.

The car park is a large grassy area at the top of the beach, so lugging your cool boxes involves only a short walk before your toes are on the sand.

FIND IT Beach Road, Winterton-on Sea (nearest postcode is NR29 4AJ).

BROCKHILL COUNTRY PARK

HYTHE, KENT

Once part of a game estate that serviced Saltwood Castle in Norman times, Brockhill Country Park is now a popular public park on the outskirts of Hythe. It has a central lake, open grassland and meadows, plus a bunch of facilities that make for an easy afternoon out with a group: toilets, play area and a dedicated picnic area with benches.

There are a few different areas to pick from for a gathering. The deer paddock is an attractive grassy area with walnut and sycamore trees. For shade, head to the pond as there are plentiful overhanging trees to cool down under or, if your party of people is truly vast, the valley in the middle of the park is the largest area to set up the blankets and cool boxes.

FIND IT Sandling Road, Hythe, Kent, CT21 4HL. There is plenty of pay-and-display parking.

DEVIL'S DYKE

BRIGHTON, EAST SUSSEX

A fabulous breath of fresh air, just 5 miles north of busy Brighton, the Dyke is the best place to take a bunch of friends needing refreshing after a night on the town. At 217m above sea level, this spot makes you feel like you are soaring with the clouds. From your picnic rug, you'll get a 360-degree-view of the Downs, the coastline and the Weald. On a clear day, you can even see the Hog's Back 31 miles away. The picture-perfect village of Ditchling on the valley floor below you looks toy-sized. Landscape lover John Constable described it as 'the grandest view in the world'. Legend has it that the Devil dug this chasm to drown the parishioners of the Weald. Or if you are more scientifically minded, it was formed naturally just over 10,000 years ago in the last ice age.

The ridge along the top of the Dyke is vast so there is never a problem finding a spot to lay your rugs for a group gathering. Bring a kite or just watch the brightly coloured canopies of the paragliders. There are a myriad of little paths heading off to hidey holes, lumps and bumps in the landscape if you prefer to be out of the way.

FIND IT Devil's Dyke car park is 2 miles north of the A27 Brighton ring road, and just off A281. Take the Hove junction from the A27 and head north (signposted to Devil's Dyke). Follow the road and keep bearing left at any junctions until you reach the Dyke (the nearest postcode is BN1 8YJ). The car park is pay-and-display but National Trust members and Blue Badge holders park for free.

JEPHSON GARDENS

LEAMINGTON SPA, WARWICKSHIRE

Places like Jephson Gardens make you reflect on how blessed we are to have such wonderful public parks and open spaces maintained for our pleasure and enjoyment. As a location to gather and feast with friends and family, Jephson has it all. The gardens stretch for 14 acres and are awash with spectacular formal floral displays, in summer and winter. There are around 140 different species of trees, a sensory garden area, boating lake and plentiful open space suitable for taking over an area to set up camp, eat and play games of rounders and football. After lunch there's the option of a walk along the river or a hunt to find the collection of sculptures.

FIND IT Nearest postcode is CV32 4AA. Parking can be found on Newbold Terrace and Newbold Street (some pay-and-display, some free). Other car parks are at St Peter's multi-storey and Rosefield Street. The park is open every day from 8am, closing time depending on the time of year.

SAVERNAKE FOREST

MARLBOUROUGH, WILTSHIRE

This is a captivating ancient forest, rich in wildlife. Some of the trees here are so old they have seen centuries of activity take place under their boughs. Savernake is home to the famous 1,000-year-old Big Belly Oak on the western edge of the forest. It is said that Henry VIII met his third wife Jane Seymour underneath it.

It was created as a designated royal hunting ground in the 12th century and is still privately owned, having been purchased by the Duke of Somerset in 1540. Today, it is leased to the Forestry Commission, which ensures public access to the paths and tracks.

It's an exciting place to visit, almost like a maze to explore. The 18th-century landscaper 'Capability' Brown created a four-mile-long Grand Avenue that effectively cut the forest in half, but devised a central circus, from which eight walks radiate through the forest. Some of these paths open out onto grassy glades, creating fabulous private zones for your get together. There are also picnic benches dotted throughout.

FIND IT The forest is about half a mile outside Marlborough (nearest postcode is SN8 4ND). There is on-site parking. There is a designated picnic site at the beginning of the Postern Hill nature trail just off the A346 at the western end of the forest.

FIRKIN POINT

LOCH LOMOND, SCOTLAND

To be honest, anywhere around Loch Lomond is going to be great. But I'd suggest Firkin Point. The views of Loch Lomond from here are superb: water in three directions and a mountain backdrop. The advantage of heading here is that it is located on the 'Old Road' so the coach parties don't tend to stop, which means it's not going to be swamped in the summer months. A particularly nice touch is that there are picnic tables positioned along the path right next to the water's edge, so younger members of the picnic party are likely to take advantage and have a paddle whilst everyone else clears away. There's a car park and facilities, making this a fabulously easy place to get together and enjoy such a stunning location. To walk off the excesses you can pick the path up directly from here and wander along to the Loch's Head.

FIND IT A82 on the shores of Loch Lomond and the Trossachs National Park. There is a pull-off with parking.

BARRICANE BEACH

WOOLACOMBE, NORTH DEVON

I'm loathe to share this secret. Unless someone told you, you wouldn't know that this perfect sun-downer beach existed around the corner from the crowd-swamped surfing beach of Woolacombe. Barricane Beach is a delightful, small cove, hugged by rocks that create a glorious sun trap, and also provide the perfect shelter from any sea breezes. There is an entrance between the rocks into the sea, which is shallow and safe for swimming, plus a series of rock pools on different levels. It's very busy with the locals on Friday and Saturday evenings in the summer, but this beach has one of the best atmospheres for picnicking with family groups.

FIND IT You can park above the beach along the road – pay at the meters (nearest postcode is EX34 7BT). Walk west from Woolacome main beach. You'll come to a small wooden hut at the top of some steps. This is Barricane. Make sure you have a willing crowd. There are quite a few steps heading down to the beach, but it's worth everyone's while to carry a bag.

4
MEALS ON WHEELS

FOR KIDS, FAMILIES AND DINNERS IN DENS

Taking children on a picnic, however simple, adds a frisson of excitement to any food. Even the fussiest of eaters seem to lose food inhibitions when it's eaten off their lap. This makes picnics the best kind of meal if you are under 10. Let's face it, you're outside, there's a spread of interesting food choices before you, no cutlery and no fuss if you drop it on the floor.

Picnics don't need to be saved for the weekend. Having your tea on a picnic rug after school in the local park ticks several boxes on the frazzled parents list of: feed, entertain and tire them before bed. Invite others to bring their own food and kids, and you've managed a bit of social time too.

Kids equal kit. Depending on their age, this means pushchairs, changing gear, wipes and toys. It's endless. So, a tip for a good picnic spot for families is: don't choose somewhere an hour's hike from the car. Pack your gear and picnic food in a pull-a-long truck (like the ones people use for their children at music festivals) or one of those granny shopping trolleys that are now trendy again. I have one, so they must be. Meals on wheels makes for an easy life.

The following recipes include portions sized for smaller hands: mini pizza puff spirals, tortilla fingers and cold chicken dippers and dips. There's a few twists and restyling of old classics: raspberry and orange oat bites (a funkier flapjack), individual jars of homemade houmous and some small appealing ideas with fruit will all hopefully entice the most reluctant of foodies.

HOUMOUS JARS

A healthy yet appealing looking snack, these personal jars of houmous can be jazzed up with ribbons, stickers or name labels depending on the age of the guests. When you realise that making your own delicious version takes less than two minutes, I think you'll forget the shop-bought variety forever.

Ingredients

400g tin chickpeas, drained

3 tsp tahini

3 tsp olive oil

2 tsp lemon juice

½ garlic clove

2 tbsp hot water

Large pinch of salt

4 small jam jars with lids (I use 185g jars)

Suggestions for crudités

3 large carrots, peeled and cut into long batons

3 celery sticks, cut in half and then cut into sticks the same size as the carrot batons

Sugar snap peas

½ cucumber, deseeded and cut into batons

Strips of red or yellow pepper (one pepper between the four is enough)

Method

Put all the houmous ingredients in a bowl and use an electric hand mixer to blend it all together to make a smooth paste. If you prefer a chunkier houmous, use the hand blender in short, sharp bursts until you get the consistency you like.

Spoon the houmous equally between the jars and put the lids on to transport them to the picnic.

A tip for preparing the crudités is to hold up the carrot next to the jar and cut the batons to a length that enables it to stick up about 4cm above the tops of the jar once you've put it in the houmous. Cut the other vegetables to the same length (but not the sugar snap peas).

Pack the crudités separately. When you are about to serve, take the lids off the jars and pack them with the crudités so that they are just touching the houmous.

Prep time: 15 minutes
Cooking time: none
Serves: 4

CHICKEN
DIPPERS & DIPS

These are delicious hot or cold so I'd suggest making double the amount at tea time the night before a picnic and get two meals for the effort of one. Depending on the palates of the picnickers, you can play around with the flavouring of the chicken coating. A sprinkle of mild chilli powder or a little garlic salt in the flour would suit more adventurous eaters.

Ingredients

2 large chicken breast fillets (350g)

2 medium eggs, lightly beaten

100ml buttermilk or whole milk

200g plain flour

1 heaped tbsp sweet smoked paprika

1 tsp sea salt

Freshly ground black pepper

Approx 600ml of rapeseed oil for frying

Honey mustard dip

3 tbsp mayonnaise

3 tbsp mild wholegrain mustard

3 tbsp runny honey

Barbecue sauce

2 tbsp Worcestershire sauce

2 tbsp ketchup

2 tbsp honey

Method

Cut each chicken breast into 3 or 4 lengths and then cut these lengths in half to create large, nugget-sized pieces.

Whisk the eggs and buttermilk in a large bowl then add the chicken pieces, making sure they are fully coated.

Put the flour, paprika, salt and pepper in a plastic tub with a lid. Take the chicken pieces out of the egg mixture, shake off any excess and put them all into the tub. Put the lid on and shake the tub so that the chicken pieces get thoroughly coated. Take them out and repeat the process: putting them in the egg and buttermilk mixture followed by the flour. Shake again.

Heat the rapeseed oil in a saucepan; you want it to be at least 4cm deep. Check it is hot enough for deep frying by dropping a small amount of the leftover egg mixture into it. If it immediately sizzles and fluffs up, it is hot enough. Don't leave the pan alone.

In batches, fry the chicken pieces for about 3 to 4 minutes on each side. The coating will turn a lovely golden brown.

Lay the fried chicken pieces on plenty of kitchen paper to soak up the excess oil while you continue to fry the rest of the chicken. When they are all done, put them on some fresh kitchen paper within an airtight tub. Chill in the fridge until ready to go.

To make the dips, simply mix the ingredients of each dip together and take in a small tub with a lid or little jam jar.

Prep time: 15 minutes
Cooking time: 20 minutes
Serves: 4

CHEESE, HAM & CORN MUFFINS

Far more interesting than a cheese and ham sandwich, these savoury muffins are still made with the same safe flavours for fussy eaters. Muffins are sometimes made with buttermilk, which is not always easy to find in the shops, so this version uses milk and natural yoghurt, and the results are surprisingly light and fluffy.

Ingredients

50g smoked ham slices

200g self-raising flour

1½ heaped tsp baking powder

Generous pinch of salt

1 tsp caster sugar

2 heaped tbsp sweetcorn

80g cheddar cheese, grated plus an extra 10g for sprinkling on the top before cooking

100g good-quality, natural yoghurt

125ml milk, whole or semi skimmed

40g salted butter, melted

1 small egg

Muffin tin lined with 8 cases

Method

Preheat the oven to 200°C/Fan 180°C/400°F/Gas mark 6.

Chop the ham into small pieces about 1cm square.

In a large bowl, mix together the self-raising flour, baking powder, salt, sugar, sweetcorn and grated cheese.

In a separate bowl, combine the yoghurt, milk, melted butter, egg and ham. It will look a little lumpy but that's fine. Give it a good mix then pour it into the bowl of flour and mix well again.

Spoon the mixture equally into the muffin cases. Sprinkle the extra cheese across the top of each muffin.

Bake in the oven for about 20 to 25 minutes until they are well risen and golden in colour.

Remove from the muffin tin immediately and leave to cool on a wire rack. Pack into an airtight container.

These are really good thickly spread with proper butter

Prep time: 15 minutes
Cooking time: 25 minutes
Makes: 8 muffins

FRESH STRAWBERRY
ROCKY ROADS

Just wow. And with the added joy of fresh strawberries, this is my best rocky road recipe yet. I've made them with half milk chocolate, half dark chocolate but feel free to adjust that ratio according to your picnickers. I once made these with all dark chocolate for an all grown-ups picnic and they went before the sandwiches.

Ingredients

100g milk chocolate

100g dark chocolate

50g mini marshmallows

30g whole blanched almonds, roughly chopped

20g walnuts or hazelnuts, roughly chopped

75g fresh strawberries

2 digestive biscuits

23cm x 12cm (2lb) loaf tin, lined

Method

Break the chocolate into small pieces and put them in a heatproof bowl placed over a saucepan of boiling water. Stir it occasionally until it has all melted. Take off the heat and put to one side.

In a separate bowl, put the mini marshmallows and the nuts.

Cut the stalks off the strawberries and cut them into small pieces about the size of the mini marshmallows; put them in the bowl too. Finally break the digestive biscuits into bite-sized pieces and add them to the bowl.

Pour in the melted chocolate and use a wooden spoon or spatula to carefully mix it all together so that all the ingredients are thoroughly coated in the chocolate.

Spoon the mixture into the loaf tin and push it down tightly, making sure it is pushed into the edges of the tin.

Cover the tin in cling film and put it in the fridge for 2 hours until it has completely set.

Use a large sharp knife to cut into squares. Pack between sheets of baking parchment to transport to the picnic.

Prep time: 15 minutes
Cooking time: 2 hours to chill
Makes: 8 squares

PIZZA PUFF SPIRALS

With simple store cupboard ingredients of tomato purée and grated cheese, these little puff pastry swirls are so easy to make I suggest getting the children to do it themselves. A bit like a mini pizza in flavour, they tend to be scoffed within minutes of appearing on the picnic rug.

Ingredients

125g ready-made puff pastry

2 tbsp tomato purée

2 tbsp pesto

75g cheddar cheese or mozzarella, grated

Method

Preheat the oven to 220°C/Fan 200°C/425°F/Gas mark 7.

Put a baking tray upside down on the top shelf. This will provide a hot surface to help cook the underside of the pastry.

Unroll the puff pastry, keeping it on the greaseproof paper that it has been rolled up in. It should be about 3mm thick, so roll it out a bit if it needs to be thinner.

Spread the tomato purée all over the pastry making sure you get good coverage, then do the same with the pesto. Sprinkle the cheese evenly across the top.

Starting at a short edge, roll the pastry up as tightly as you can. Wrap the roll in cling film and chill in the fridge for about 30 minutes until it has firmed up a little.

When ready to bake remove the cling film and cut the roll into 12 slices. Place the pieces, cut side down, on a baking tray lined with baking parchment. Put this on the heated upturned baking tray in the oven for 15 minutes until the spirals have risen and turned golden brown.

Transfer to a wire rack to cool. Pack in between layers of kitchen paper to transport to your picnic.

Prep time: 10 minutes
Cooking time: 15 to 18 minutes
Makes: 12 spirals

RASPBERRY & ORANGE
OAT BITES

Raspberry and orange make a gorgeous flavour combination in these oat-based bites. These moreish squares won't last long, but the resulting energy burst from the oats and nuts will, so make sure you get the kids running around afterwards.

Ingredients

200g plain flour

200g porridge oats

200g unsalted butter, softened and cut into small pieces

50g hazelnuts or almonds, crushed

175g light brown sugar

Zest of 1 orange, finely grated

100g pine nuts

150g fresh raspberries

23cm square shallow baking tin, greased and lined with baking parchment

Method

Preheat the oven to 190°C/Fan 170°C/375°F/Gas mark 5.

Put the flour and oats in a mixing bowl and use your fingers to rub the butter in to make big lumpy crumbs.

Mix in the crushed hazelnuts, sugar, orange zest and two-thirds of the pine nuts. Spoon two-thirds of the crumbly mixture into the tin, spread it out and press it down lightly.

Spread the raspberries across the top of this, crush them down slightly with the back of a fork so that they 'squidge' a little, then sprinkle the rest of the oat mixture on the top and finally the remaining pine nuts.

Use the back of a spoon to press the mixture down lightly all over.

Bake in the oven on the middle shelf for about 35 minutes until it has turned golden on the top.

Leave to cool in the tin. Cut into 12 squares and pack between baking parchment.

Prep time: 15 minutes
Cooking time: 35 minutes
Makes: 12 squares

RED PEPPER
TORTILLA FINGERS

This can be made with a variety of different ingredients along with the potatoes, such as sun-dried tomatoes, peas, ham, flakes of white fish and fresh herbs. In fact, it's a good way of sneaking in new ingredients that younger children might otherwise not choose. You can use a diced, fresh red pepper, rather than from a jar, but fry it with the onion to soften it.

Ingredients

270g white potato, peeled and cut into 1cm cubes

15g unsalted butter

1 small onion, finely chopped

2 roasted red peppers from a jar, drained and cut into 1cm pieces

6 large eggs

2 tbsp double cream or milk

Pinch of ground nutmeg

Salt and black pepper

2 tbsp grated cheddar cheese

20cm frying pan with a heatproof handle

Method

Cook the potatoes in boiling salted water until just tender (about 5 minutes) then put to one side to cool.

Melt the butter in the frying pan and gently sauté the onion on a low heat for about 8 minutes, until it softens.

Add the potatoes and gently fry for another 5 minutes. Stir occasionally so that they cook all over and don't catch on the bottom of the pan. Add the peppers and mix gently, then take off the heat.

In a separate bowl, beat the eggs with the cream and pinch of nutmeg and give it a good seasoning with the salt and pepper. Add the cheese and mix it in.

Pour this over the potato, onion and pepper mixture in the frying pan and leave it on a low heat until it is almost set. This will take about 10 minutes. Carefully run a knife around the edge halfway through cooking to help prevent it sticking. The middle of the top will still be a little runny, but the rest of the egg should be set.

Preheat the grill to a medium heat. Place the frying pan under the grill until the top has set and has browned slightly. Allow it to cool for about 10 minutes before turning it out onto a board or plate.

Cut it into finger-width wedges and pack for the picnic.

Prep time: 25 minutes
Cooking time: 15 minutes
Serves: 8

CRUNCHY RED, WHITE & GREEN
PASTA SALAD

Discovering crunchy, cheesy croutons in this pasta salad makes it a hit with all the children I've served it to. I've baked the croutons with parmesan cheese but you could sprinkle them with dried mixed herbs to give them a pizza-style flavour instead. Take the croutons in a separate, airtight container to keep them crunchy, and serve them at the last minute.

Ingredients

2 slices white bread, crusts cut off

1 large garlic clove

Olive oil cooking spray, or use a pastry brush dipped in oil

2 tbsp parmesan, finely grated

200g farfalle pasta

2 tbsp olive oil, plus a little for drizzling

1 tsp honey

1 tbsp red wine vinegar

Salt and black pepper

150g cherry tomatoes of different colours if possible, halved

150g mini mozzarella balls

1 ripe avocado, cut into cubes

Juice of ½ lemon

Handful of fresh basil leaves

Method

Preheat the oven to 150°C/Fan 130°C/300°F/Gas mark 2.

To make the croutons, cut the garlic clove in half and rub the cut edge across the slices of bread on each side.

Cut the bread into small cubes about the size of a sugar cube and spread them out on a baking tray. Spray them lightly with oil, turning the cubes so that they get a little touch of oil all over. Don't soak them. Alternatively, dip a pastry brush in some oil and lightly brush over the cubes.

Put the tray in the oven for 10 minutes. Take the tray out and turn the cubes, sprinkle the parmesan over them and put back in for another 10 minutes until they are crisp and golden brown. Put to one side to cool.

Cook the pasta according to instructions. Drain and rinse under cold water and drain again, then drizzle a little oil through it, mix and put to one side to cool.

Whisk together the olive oil, honey, red wine vinegar and some salt and pepper. Pour this over the tomatoes and mozzarella balls, then add it into the pasta and mix. Pack in a sealable tub.

Put the cut avocado in a separate tub and squeeze the lemon juice over the top with some black pepper, or take the avocado whole and cut it just before it's needed. To serve, mix the avocado, croutons and torn up basil leaves through the pasta.

Prep time: 10 minutes
Cooking time: 30 minutes
Serves: 4

SUPER SMOOTHIES & JOLLY JUICES

These drinks are a great way of getting a good shot of fresh fruit into an otherwise cake-frenzied bunch of picnickers. You will need a blender or electric hand-blender to make these.

WATERMELON & MINT COOLER

This is a good way of using up the leftover watermelon from the watermelon wheel on page 158 or the halloumi salad on page 220. Don't make it too far in advance as you want some fizz left in your lemonade.

Ingredients

400g fresh watermelon, deseeded and chopped up into small pieces

600ml lemonade

12 fresh mint leaves

Method

Put all of the ingredients into the blender and whizz it until smooth and frothy. You may have to do this in a couple of batches. Pour immediately into a flask, add a handful of ice cubes and seal the lid, ready for when you head out the door.

BANANA & MANGO SMOOTHIE

This tropical treat is a naturally thick and creamy smoothie. If you think the palates will be obliging, you can add slices of tinned or fresh pineapple too.

Ingredients

4 bananas, peeled and sliced

250g or 1 large, ripe mango, peeled and cut into chunks

250ml orange juice

4 tsp honey

Method

Put all the ingredients together in a blender and blitz. Alternatively, mash the banana and mango together with the back of the fork. Mix in the honey and then use a whisk while you pour in the orange juice. Whisk until the drink is smooth. Pour into a flask, pop in a couple of ice cubes and seal until you need it.

Prep time: 10 minutes,
20 minutes for lemonade
Serves: 4

SUMMER BERRY SMOOTHIE

Thick, nourishing and filling, this one uses milk and yoghurt. Only make this if you are going to be able to keep it cool, though using frozen berries will help with that.

Ingredients

400g bag frozen mixed summer berries

250ml whole milk

250g strawberry or raspberry yoghurt

2 tbsp runny honey

Method

Use a blender to whizz all of the ingredients together and decant into a flask. Store in a cool bag next to ice blocks.

PINK LEMONADE

This drink's got a glorious tang to it, sweetened by the raspberries. Just add more sugar to achieve the right 'sweet tooth' level for your diners.

Ingredients

300g caster sugar

170g fresh raspberries

1½ lemons, sliced

Sprig of fresh mint

Bottle of still or sparkling water

Method

Put the sugar, raspberries, lemon slices and a mint leaf into a saucepan and add 350ml of *tap* water.

Bring to the boil, while slowly stirring. Let it bubble for 5 minutes, then turn the heat off and leave the liquid to cool.

Pour through a sieve and use the back of a spoon to push and scrape all of the juice out of the bits of fruit. Store the syrup in a fridge.

When you are ready to serve, pour the syrup into the bottom of four glasses and top up with sparking or still water.

Pop a couple of fresh raspberries and a couple of mint leaves on the top.

STICKY SWEET
SESAME SAUSAGES

This recipe is virtually effort free, but with no compromises on taste. I've given quantities for three chipolatas each for hungry children, though if you're my husband all 12 would count as one complete serving, so just increase all amounts accordingly. And let's face it, you can't have a picnic without a cold sausage. It's not right.

Ingredients

12 good-quality pork chipolatas

6 tbsp honey

3 tbsp sesame oil

3 tbsp soy sauce

3 tbsp sesame seeds

Method

Preheat the oven to 190°C/Fan 170°C/375°F/Gas mark 5.

Cook the sausages for 10 to 15 minutes, until they are just beginning to brown.

While they are cooking, whisk together the honey, sesame oil and soy sauce in a large bowl.

When the sausages are done, tip them into the marinade and mix them about so they all get coated.

Take them out one by one, shake off the excess marinade and put them back on the baking tray. A top tip here is to line the baking tray with a sheet of greaseproof paper as the sugar in the honey tends to burn on the bottom and makes it harder to clean.

Sprinkle the sausages with the sesame seeds and put back into the oven for about 15 minutes. Keep an eye on them so the honey doesn't burn.

Take them out of the oven and leave to cool, then stack on layers of greaseproof paper to prevent sticking and chill for at least a couple of hours in the fridge.

Prep time: 5 minutes
Cooking time: 30 minutes
Serves: 4

CINNAMON
BUTTER POPCORN

A big bowl of this spiced, buttery popcorn placed in the middle of a picnic rug is always a winner. It's one of the quickest things to make, so this is a good one if you are prepping for a last-minute picnic.

Ingredients

150g unpopped popping corn

2 tbsp flavourless vegetable or rapeseed oil

75g salted butter

3 heaped tbsp brown sugar

1 tsp ground cinnamon

Method

To make the popcorn, add the oil to a large saucepan with a lid and heat it over a high heat for 3 minutes.

Drop a couple of corn kernels into the oil to see if they pop to check whether it is ready for the rest of the corn.

If so, tip the rest of the kernels in and quickly cover with the lid. Keep shaking the pan so that the corn kernels keep moving and don't burn.

Put some good music on and continue to shake until the rate of popping starts to slow down and stop. Transfer the popped corn to a large bowl, picking out the unpopped kernels.

Melt the butter in a separate saucepan, add the sugar and the cinnamon and keep stirring until all of the sugar has dissolved.

Pour this over the popcorn and mix until it is all coated. Leave it to cool. You can put the popcorn into separate bags as individual portions, or in a large sealable bag or tub to transport it and serve in a big bowl at the picnic.

Prep time: 5 minutes
Cooking time: 15 minutes
Serves: 4

FUNKY FRUIT

Sweet, beautiful and colourful. Fruit in its natural state is far more exciting than anything we could cook with it. Or at least this is what we need to tell the kids. All I've done here is arrange it to raise a few smiles.

WATERMELON WHEEL

Ingredients

2 whole slices of watermelon, taken from the plumpest part of the fruit

16 lolly sticks

Method

Cut each slice into eight wedges and put lolly sticks into the skins for easy grabbing. To help put the lolly sticks in, carefully make a slit in the skin with a very sharp paring knife. Stack the watermelon wedges for transporting in a plastic tub then arrange into wheels on a board at the picnic.

This quantity allows for 4 wedges each.

RAINBOW POTS

Ingredients

240g strawberries, cut into quarters

240g green grapes, cut in half

280g clementine segments, cut in half

200g fresh pineapple, chopped into small pieces

240g blueberries

4 x 50cl see-through cups

Method

Simply layer the berries, grapes, pineapple and clementines into the cups. Obviously you can change the types of fruit used, just make sure you get a variety of colours to get the right impact. Avoid things that will go brown like chopped apple or banana.

Prep time: 15 minutes each
Cooking time: none
Serves: 4

PIGGY-IN-THE-MIDDLE SANDWICH LOAF

Full of surprises, this foccacia-style bread has the filling baked into it. Use flavours that you know your children will enjoy; I've used ham (hence Piggy-in-the-Middle) and cheese. The trick is to not use fillings that have too much moisture – so no fresh tomatoes as the bread will go soggy. It takes a while to make but it's the most fabulous and perfect picnic loaf.

Ingredients

For the bread

250g strong white bread flour

1 tsp salt

½ tsp caster sugar

1 x 7g sachet of easy blend bread yeast

1 tbsp olive oil

200ml cold water

Extra olive oil for drizzling

For the filling

100g cheddar or mozzarella cheese

150g wafer-thin ham

8 sun-dried tomatoes, patted dry using kitchen paper ➤→

Method

Put the flour, salt, sugar, yeast and olive oil into a large bowl and add 150ml of water. Give it a good stir with a wooden spoon and then get your hands in to bring it together to become a dough. While you are doing this, gradually pour in a little more water from the remaining 50ml and keep kneading it with your other hand. You might not need to use all of the water as you don't want it to go sticky.

Get the dough out onto a floured surface and start kneading it properly, stretching and pushing with the heel of your hand, folding it over, stretching it again, giving it a quarter turn and repeating the pushing, stretching and folding.

Do this for about 8 minutes.

Drizzle a little oil in the bottom of a clean bowl, place the dough into it and cover with a tea towel. Leave in a warm place for an hour. After this time, it should have doubled in size.

Tip the dough out onto a lined baking tray and use your hands to stretch it out into roughly a rectangular shape as big as your baking tray.

On one side of the rectangle put a layer of ham, followed by some slices of cheese and sun-dried tomatoes and repeat to use all the filling. Then fold the side without the filling over the top as if you are closing a book. ➤→

Prep time: 25 minutes
Cooking time: 20 minutes
(2 hours proving) Serves: 4

PIGGY-IN-THE-MIDDLE
SANDWICH LOAF

For the topping

12 mozzarella balls

2 tbsp pesto

4 sun-dried tomatoes, each cut
into 3 pieces

4 slices of parma ham, each
sliced into 4 rough squares

Drizzle of olive oil

Sea salt flakes

Sprigs of thyme or rosemary

Move the dough into the middle of the tray and push the dough down again. Seal the edges by squeezing them together.

Cover with a tea towel and leave to prove for another half an hour. It should have puffed up again.

Now for the topping. Dip a mozzarella ball in the pesto, place a piece of sun-dried tomato on the top and put this on top of a square of ham. Push this little stack down into the dough on the top of the loaf. Repeat this so that you have 12 pesto/mozzarella/ ham/tomato balls across the loaf. Cover it again with the tea towel and leave to prove for another 40 minutes.

Preheat the oven to 220°C/Fan 200°C/425°F/Gas mark 7 and put an upturned baking tray on the top shelf.

Drizzle the loaf with a little oil, sprinkle with sea salt flakes and place a few thyme sprigs across the top. Put it on the tray in the oven for 20 minutes, until a golden crust has formed and the bottom sounds hollow when you tap it.

MENU IDEAS

1 Cheese, ham and corn muffins | Sticky sweet sesame sausages | Red pepper tortilla fingers | Raspberry and orange oat bites | Super smoothies

Young family fun: a few bits to grab and go, and to graze on.

2 Chicken dippers and dips | Red, white and green pasta salad | Funky fruit rainbow pots | Orange zest brownies

For after-school tea in the park.

3 Piggy-in-the-middle picnic loaf | Grown-up sausage roll | Chicken dippers and dips | Spinach and ricotta boreks | Banana and blueberry loaf cake | Chocolate, orange and pine nut cookies | Super smoothies

This one is for older kids, days out on the mountain bikes and family hikes.

4 Gin-baked salmon | Orzo primavera salad | Sticky sweet sesame sausages | Pizza puff spirals | Sunny salad | Smoked cheese straws | Cheese, ham and corn muffins | Strawberry rocky roads | Rose meringues | Houmous jars | Funky fruit | Cinnamon butter popcorn

A large gathering of families and food for all ages.

MARVELLOUS PLACES

FOR THE

PERFECT FAMILY PICNIC

—— DALBY FOREST ——

YORKSHIRE

Dalby Forest on the southern slopes of the North Yorkshire Moors National Park is a brilliant day out for children and adults. Managed by the Forestry Commission, the focus is on activity, so if you have a bunch of children you want to wear out before filling their bellies – this is the right place to come. The landscape is varied, with cycling trails across hills and dales, through thick forest and across moorland plateaus. There is tree climbing and zip-lining and oodles of open space to run and chase a ball. There's even a Gruffalo walking trail.

Clearly the picnic spot opportunities are endless. A great one is the Adderstone Field play area. You can park the car right next to it, there is a big open space for running around, playing frisbee and football, as well as an adventure play area too. There is also easy access from here for the Gruffalo trail and the Enchanted Forest walk.

FIND IT Forestry Commission visitor centre, Low Dalby, Thornton-le-Dale, Pickering, North Yorkshire, YO18 7LT. Dalby Forest is two miles northeast of Thornton-le-Dale, and can also be reached via the A169 Pickering to Whitby road. Look out for the brown tourist signs. Admission by car to Dalby Forest is via a toll road, but free for cyclists and walkers. Follow signs to Adderstone Field play area.

—— VERULAMIUM PARK ——

ST ALBANS

Set in more than 100 acres of beautiful parkland in the centre of St Albans, this is a gorgeous place for both peace and play at your picnic, depending on where you park the picnic trolley. There is a big family picnic area, a lake with ducks, and the River Ver running through the middle if you prefer to find some calm by the water. But what makes this place stand out is that it is bursting with Roman remains. The park is named after the Roman city of Verulamium on which it stands. St Albans lays claim to being one of the oldest settlements in the UK. Take a stroll around the park with the children and you'll find large sections of the Roman city wall still intact, and a well-preserved mosaic that once formed part of a large town house. There is also a free museum in the middle of the park, with hands-on displays to bring it all to life.

If your kids are more excited by modern facilities, there's the free splash park open during the summer months (it gets busy!). It's a huge series of open-air paddling pools and water sprays. The splash park itself is gated, but you can sit right next to it on your picnic rug. There are large trees that surround the splash area so there is shade if you need it.

FIND IT Verulamium Park car park, 39 St Michael's Street, St Albans, AL3 4SW.

— WHISBY NATURE PARK —

LINCOLN

Whisby Nature Park is a beautiful landscape near Lincoln. Once a barren deserted quarry, it is now full of wildlife, walking trails and places to stop and soak up the sights and sounds of nature. The quarry pits have been filled with water and are home to a variety of birds and water creatures. You can learn all about them in the Natural World Centre where kids can get hands on with the displays.

The nature park is free to visit and children are made welcome. There are plenty of nature activities to get involved in as well as the fantastic Little Darters' play area near the Natural World Centre. This amazing structure stretches over the water onto an island and is loaded with lookout towers, earth tunnels, big sand pits and a mole's-eye view pod for watching mini beasts up close, as well as climbing nets, rope bridges and water chutes. There is a designated picnic area and facilities near the Natural World Centre.

FIND IT Moor Lane, Thorpe-on-the-Hill, LN6 9BW.

— RUMBLING KERN —

NORTHUMBERLAND

Rumbling Kern Beach, near Howick in Northumberland, is fondly known as Rocky Seaside to the locals. Rumbling Kern was once the haunt of whisky smugglers hauling their contraband up the beach, today it is a charming but secretive cove worthy of a picnic with the kids.

A walk down a little farm track from the parking area brings you out onto a small beach in a rocky bay south of Cullernose Point. The sandy beach is sheltered behind small cliffs that face inland from the sea providing shelter from the gusty North Sea breezes that come as standard on the dramatic Northumberland coast.

You won't see many other people, the most obvious sign of life being the charming Grade II listed bathing house that sits on the rock above the beach. It was built in the 19th century by Charles Grey, 2nd Earl Grey (who was Prime Minister between 1830 and 1834). He had 16 children and the house was built for the family to go bathing. Lady Grey used to sit in the upstairs window and watch the children bathe.

The sandy cove is safe for small children to play in, while the rocks provide a natural climbing frame for the older ones. The bonus is that your picnic rug is sheltered from the wind so you can keep the sand out of your picnic.

FIND IT From the Alnwick bypass (A1) take the B1340 turn off at Denwick and follow signs to Longhoughton. At Longhoughton follow the B1339 north and after a mile, turn right towards Howick. There's a parking area just by Sea Houses farm where the road turns sharp left along the coast. The track just north of the farm leads to the cove.

HAM HILL COUNTRY PARK

SOUTH SOMERSET

One of the best places to run up and down hills, hide in hamstone crevices and make dens in the woods. Local kids often refer to the landscape in Ham Hill Country Park as being 'like the moon'. An undulating series of hilly mounds were left behind by Victorian quarrying. The mounds are now covered in grass and provide a habitat for a wealth of butterflies, birds and insects. In the summer, it's a palette of yellows, whites, reds and purples as the wildflowers take over. This is the only place in the world where you can find hamstone, the beautiful golden rock from which the area is formed. On top of the hill, you can look out across the Somerset levels, and see the surrounding villages, all built from the same golden stone. There are so many places to set up a feast for the family here. Find a den within a little valley between the rocky mounds, or head to the woods, which have many dappled dells to make your own.

FIND IT Ham Hill Country Park, Stoke Sub Hamdon, Somerset, TA14 6RW. From the A303 turn off for Crewkerne and Stoke sub Hamdon on the A356 then follow the brown signs to Ham Hill.

HAUGHMOND HILL

SHREWSBURY

On the outskirts of Shrewsbury in Shropshire, this is an ideal spot for a gentle family walk or some off-road cycling if that's more your style. A partly wooded hill, there are some truly impressive views across the River Severn and the historic town of Shrewsbury. So if you fancy a picnic with a view, this is a great one.

The hill is managed by the Forestry Commission, who have done a great job in updating the site to make it attractive and accessible to families. There are information boards (at child height) and walks are graded by length and difficultly ranging from a mile to two miles. Two of the paths are suitable for pushchairs.

It's a natural playground, with fallen logs for balancing on, rocks to find and sticks to throw – there are plenty of places to stop and sit down for a picnic in the dappled sunlight. There are more picnic benches in an attractive setting near the parking area if you don't want to carry everything too far – and of course there are toilets.

FIND IT Follow the B5062 from Shrewsbury to Newport. Keep an eye out for Haughmond Quarry sign. Don't turn into the Quarry, but take the next right after that. Keep going down the lane and you'll see the entrance to the car park on the right.

—— OTTERS POOL ——

GALLOWAY FOREST PARK

Known as 'the highlands of the lowlands', Galloway Forest Park offers impressive views and diverse, dramatic scenery stretching from coast to mountain peak. Set in the heart of Galloway, southern Scotland, this 300-square-mile-stretch of wild beauty (managed by the Forestry Commission Scotland) is Britain's largest forest park.

Naturally, there are many places to enjoy a picnic, but a great option, close enough to your car to wheel your meal, is Otters Pool – a wide stretch of shallow river with plentiful stepping stones and easy rocks to hop and clamber on.

It is located on one of two marked forest drives that are open to vehicles between April and October. Starting at the Clatteringshaws visitor centre, Raiders Road is a 10-mile drive. It's a perfect way to see the park's woods and wildlife without having to walk too far. Stop and park up at Otters Pool (half way along) and within a few easy steps you'll find a perfect riverside picnic spot on the play-friendly grassy banks. There is a lovely stone sculpture of an otter here too, one of many contemporary works of art in the surrounding area.

FIND IT Head to Clatteringshaws visitor centre, New Galloway, Castle Douglas, DG7 3SQ to pick up Raiders Road towards Otters Pool. There are toilets and picnic benches at the Otters Pool car park area.

—— YORKSHIRE SCULPTURE PARK ——

WEST BRETTON, WAKEFIELD

You can add a cultural twist to your family picnic at the wonderful Yorkshire Sculpture Park. There are 80 works of art dotted around the 500 acres of parkland, creating a wonderland for the imaginations of old and young. Finding the sculptures is like hunting for hidden treasures, and unlike in traditional galleries you can touch many of the artworks. There is a musical sculpture called *Playground* that is particularly popular with children, as well as the half-woman, half-hare sculpture *Crawling* by Sophie Ryder, made from casts of plastic toys. Families can also take a walk around the lakes and surrounding woodland dotted with bridges, follies, a Greek-style summer house, a now land-locked boat house, stepping stones and a magical shell grotto. Picnics are welcome anywhere in the grounds. There is no entrance fee, just a parking charge.

FIND IT Yorkshire Sculpture Park is 7 miles outside of Wakefield and 20 miles south of Leeds in West Yorkshire. The best postcode for sat nav is WF4 4JX. Exit the M1 at junction 38, take the A637 towards Huddersfield, and follow the Yorkshire Sculpture Park brown heritage signs for one mile until you reach a roundabout. Turn left at the roundabout and follow the road through to the YSP car park.

—— MINERS WELFARE PARK ——

BEDWORTH, WARWICKSHIRE

Found to the south of the market town of Bedworth, this park comes with a bit of local history. The Miners Welfare Park was opened in 1925, built on reclaimed colliery land and dedicated to the local public by the miners who had worked there. It is now a great place to take the children of all ages. There is a state-of-the-art play area with water play, sand pit and a sensory section. For the older ones, there is a skate park, outdoor gym and miles of tarmac paths for scooters and bikes (and pushchairs). When they have exhausted themselves thoroughly, you can lay your rug near the fishing lake and wildflower area in the southern part of the park for a bit of respite.

FIND IT Miners Welfare Park, Rye Piece Ringway, Bedworth, CV12 8JT. You can get 3 hours free parking in Bedworth leisure centre, which is part of the park. There are also toilets here.

—— NEW FOREST ——

HAMPSHIRE

The New Forest National Park is a vast and varied landscape covering around 220 square miles. Calling it a 'forest' is actually a bit of a misnomer as a large part of it is heather-covered heathland. There are also streams, wide lawns, rivers, picturesque villages and of course plenty of stunning ancient woodland.

This variety is why it is such a good place to take a picnic. Depending on mood or occasion, it provides remote forest spots to enjoy a meal on the move if you are walking or cycling, wide open spaces for large family gatherings, characterful hidey-holes among the ferns and plenty of babbling brooks and streams that are safe for dipping toes and even sitting in. They invariably come with a rope swing as standard.

Linford Bottom is an exciting natural playground of shallow streams for paddling, gorse hedges that double up as mazes to run between and trees to climb. Groups of happy picnickers can find little secluded spots to lay out their rugs and feast without encroaching on each others' space. The only interruption you are likely to get is from some of the New Forest ponies or cattle that roam freely here. They are as much a feature of this area as the trees or gorse and are part of its magic. However, the park authorities request that you never share your sausage rolls (or any other part of your picnic) with the ponies. As if you would. Linford Bottom is an easy walk from the car park.

FIND IT Head for Linford Bottom car park. From the eastbound A31 to head towards Poulner Hill (away from Ringwood). When you get almost to the top of the hill, there is a nursery/garden centre on the left. Go past this and then take the next turn left onto a narrow side road to head towards Shobley and ultimately to the car park at Linford Bottom. Get there early in the summer holidays to bag a space.

5
POSH HAMPERS

FOR HIGH DAYS, HOLIDAYS AND BANQUETS ON BLANKETS

This chapter is about pulling out the stops. There are many life events that warrant a banquet on a blanket: birthdays, anniversaries or a Proms in the Park type event, of which there are plenty to choose from in the summer months. National Trust properties and other estates across the country host busy schedules of open air theatre, fireworks and music. Take full advantage of having access to these delightful heritage estates with their formal gardens and acres of parkland. You can soak up the grandeur of their multi-million pound properties by hosting a fine feast in the grounds for the price of an entrance fee.

When I think of posh picnics I summon up the image of privileged types in period dramas, dining on manicured lawns with the full caboodle: chairs, tables, candelabras and the kitchen sink, all carted across the lawn by a butler, of course.

While this might not be quite the standard we'll achieve, there's no harm in trying. When going posh, pack knives, forks and wine glasses as a minimum, consider a table centrepiece for good measure and you'll feel like you're living a scene out of *Brideshead Revisited* before you've popped the first cork.

We all know how to make a cucumber sandwich, so the recipes in this chapter require a little more effort and planning, but that's the point if you are creating a refined feast for a wicker hamper. Think sophisticated, perhaps even dainty and, of course, a little bit boozy. The scarlet twice-cured gin salmon is a beautiful centrepiece, gazpacho soup served in teacups makes an easy but perfectly posh starter for a summer's evening and the simple but effective summer berry puddings are a delight.

FRENCH BEAN & PEA SALAD

Make a great dressing and the simplest of ingredients will give you a stunning salad. Who knew green beans could taste so wonderful cold? The cooked anchovies add a deep, savoury salty note, while the peas give a delightful pop of sweetness. I love the almonds in it too – every salad is improved with a bit of something crunchy.

Ingredients

400g French beans, trimmed

170g frozen peas

40g flaked almonds

2 tbsp olive oil

2 tbsp lemon juice

2 large garlic cloves, sliced thinly lengthways

5 tinned anchovies

Black pepper

1 tsp sesame seeds (optional)

Method

Put the French beans in a pan of boiling, salted water for about 4 minutes. Then add the peas, making sure the water comes back to the boil quickly, and cook the beans and peas together for 2 minutes. Both should retain some bite.

Drain the beans and peas straightaway and refresh them by running them under cold water until they are cold. Drain them again and put to one side.

In a dry frying pan, toast the flaked almonds until they start to brown a little. Tip them onto a plate to cool.

Put the olive oil into the frying pan, add the slices of garlic and anchovies and heat on low for about 2 minutes until the anchovies break up and melt.

Take it off the heat and let it cool a little. Add the lemon juice and season well with black pepper (the anchovies will provide the saltiness) and whisk together to make a dressing.

Pour this over the cooked beans and peas and toss to dress the vegetables.

Scatter in the toasted almonds and sesame seeds (if using) and put into a container for transporting.

To make a more substantial dish, try adding feta cheese

Prep time: 10 minutes
Cooking time: 15 minutes
Serves: 4 (6 as a side)

BOOZY BERRY
PICNIC PUDDINGS

These berry bombs look like you've made far more of an effort than you actually have. This recipe is easy-on-the-eye and easy-on-the-pocket, as you can buy bags of mixed frozen berries cheaply. Serve them just before you eat them by turning them out onto a plate and adding a big dollop of clotted cream on the top. Just don't forget the plates and spoons.

Ingredients

500g mixed summer berries such as blackberries, red currants, strawberries and raspberries

100ml fruit liqueur, dessert wine or gin

75g caster sugar

Approx 12 slices of day-old white bread

Clotted cream, to serve

4 ramekin dishes

A cookie cutter a little larger than the base of the ramekins

Method

Put the berries, sugar and alcohol into a saucepan to heat it through gently on a low heat. After about 3 minutes all the deep red juices will be released. Take it off the heat and leave for about 30 minutes to cool and let the flavours combine.

Put a sieve over a bowl, pour the fruit into the sieve and leave it for about 15 minutes for all the juice to drain.

Line the ramekin dishes with cling film. Use the cookie cutter to cut eight rounds out of the slices of bread. Dip four in the bowl of juice and press them into the bottom of the ramekin dishes.

Cut strips from the bread that you can use around the inside edges of the dishes. Soak these in the juices too before using them to line the dishes. Divide the berries equally between the ramekins, packing them in tightly and put the final four bread rounds, soaked in juice, on the top.

Wrap each dish tightly in cling film and chill in the fridge for at least 30 minutes.

To serve, remove the cling film and place a small plate on the top of a ramekin dish, flip it over and slide the pudding out. Add your dollops of clotted cream.

Prep time: 50 minutes
Cooking time: 30 minutes to chill
Serves: 4

JEWELLED
COUS COUS SALAD

Looks, sounds and tastes posh, but is dead easy to throw together. My #picnicwin. This delicious cous cous salad is a perfect side dish for the scarlet salmon or the pork and apricot tart.

Ingredients

20g unsalted butter, plus extra for dotting on the cous cous

1 tsp soft brown sugar

40g pecans, halved

250g cous cous

½ tsp stock powder

60g dried cranberries, or sultanas if you can't get cranberries

5 sun-dried tomatoes, chopped into small pieces

Zest of ½ orange, plus 2 tbsp orange juice

Salt and black pepper

Olive oil

Seeds from ½ a pomegranate

1 tbsp coriander, finely chopped

1 tbsp mint, finely chopped

Method

In a frying pan, melt the butter, turn the heat down low and add the brown sugar. As it begins to melt, add the pecan halves and toss them around in the mixture for about 2 minutes. Take them out of the pan and put to one side to dry by spreading out on a piece of baking parchment.

Put the dried cranberries (or sultanas) and sun-dried tomatoes in a heatproof bowl and tip the dried cous cous over the top.

Sprinkle the stock powder into the bowl along with the orange zest, orange juice and a generous seasoning of salt and pepper. Mix it thoroughly.

Drizzle the olive oil over the top and add a couple of small knobs of butter. Then pour boiling water over the cous cous until the water covers the surface by about 1cm. Cover the bowl with a plate and leave for 8 minutes.

When the time is up, put the cous cous in a serving bowl and use a fork to break up all of the grains. Mix the chopped herbs, pomegranate seeds and pecans through it, keeping a few of each back to decorate.

A great way to serve this is to pack it down into a bowl and cover with cling film. When you get to your picnic, take off the cling film, put a plate on the top of the bowl and flick it over so that the cous cous comes out as a dome. Pop some pomegranate seeds and pecans on the top and listen to the oohs and aahs.

Prep time: 25 minutes
Cooking time: 5 minutes
Serves: 4

SCARLET SALMON
TWICE-CURED BEETROOT, GIN & HERB GRAVLAX

This centrepiece is a beauty to behold. I have my friend Aussie Sarah to thank for this. As she points out, the list of ingredients looks long, but look again and you'll realise it's just a visit to the fresh herb and spice section of the supermarket. It requires planning as the salmon needs a few days (yes, days) in the fridge to cure, but it's so worth it for the wows.

Ingredients

800 to 900g salmon fillet, depending on the guests' appetites

First cure: beetroot and gin

2 fresh beetroots

2 juniper berries, crushed

2 tbsp or 1 small bunch of chopped dill

Zest of 2 unwaxed lemons, and juice of 1

Zest and juice of 1 orange

6 tbsp rock salt (use the chunky stuff, not the flakes)

2 tbsp demerara sugar

50ml gin ➻→

Method

Peel the beetroot and blitz with the juniper berries, dill, lemon zest and juice, orange zest and juice in a food processer, until it becomes a paste. Transfer the paste to a bowl and mix in the salt, sugar and gin.

Cut the salmon lengthways down the middle so you're left with 2 long, skinny pieces of salmon.

Place one piece of salmon skin side down on a piece of baking parchment on a baking tray.

Slowly spoon or pour the beetroot cure over the salmon and press down with a spoon or spatula.

Place the remaining piece of salmon on top, flesh side down, so you have effectively got a sandwich with the salmon on the top and bottom, and the cure as the sandwich filling.

Put a piece of baking parchment on top of the salmon then wrap the whole tray with cling film. Rest it in the fridge for 24 hours.

After 24 hours, gently unwrap the salmon and carefully rinse the beetroot cure off using a little cold water (or gin) to reveal the most gloriously coloured salmon. ➻→

Prep time: 1 hour 45 minutes
Cure time: 4 days
Serves: 8

181

-SCARLET SALMON-
TWICE-CURED BEETROOT, GIN & HERB GRAVLAX

Second cure: gin, herbs and horseradish

50g coarse sea salt

35g caster sugar

½ tbsp white peppercorns, crushed

½ tbsp pink peppercorns, crushed

4 tbsp or large handful of dill, finely chopped

4 tbsp or large handful of tarragon, leaves only and finely chopped

2 tbsp or small handful of parsley, finely chopped

3 tbsp horseradish sauce

50ml gin

Next lay a piece of cling fling across a baking tray, leaving extra length on either side to eventually wrap over the salmon. Put a slightly smaller piece of baking parchment on top of the cling film. The parchment needs to be just big enough to lay the salmon on.

Place one piece of the salmon, skin side down, onto the baking parchment.

Make the second cure by mixing all of the ingredients together in a bowl and covering the salmon in the same way as before – spreading the cure over one piece of salmon and placing the other, flesh side down, on top.

Place another piece of baking parchment on the top and this time wrap the salmon really tightly in the cling film, without including the baking tray. Try to avoid any air getting into your cling film parcel.

Put it back in the fridge and turn it over every 12 hours for 36 hours.

After that, your salmon is perfectly cured. Scrape off the herby paste leaving just a hint of herbs on the salmon and reveal the gorgeous dark red beneath. Slice as finely as possible, laying the slices on greaseproof paper in an airtight container.

Serve the salmon with blinis, fresh bread or just on its own with the homemade horseradish cream on page 246.

SOPHISTICATED SHORTBREAD

For me, using flowers in food has associations with refined 18th-century banquets, where fashionable ladies ate delicate morsels decorated with crystallised violets. These lavender biscuits are my version of that. Add in the lemon zest and you've got a summer's day right there in your mouth.

Ingredients

125g salted butter

50g golden caster sugar, plus extra for dusting

Zest of ¼ large unwaxed lemon

1 tsp fresh lavender flowers

125g plain flour

60g corn flour

6cm round, fluted cookie cutter

Method

Preheat the oven to 170°C/Fan 150°C/340°F/Gas mark 3.

Cream the butter and sugar together using an electric mixer. Add the lemon zest and lavender flowers and use the mixer to combine it all together.

Sift the plain flour and the corn flour together and add this gradually to the creamed butter and sugar while the mixer is on. Turn off the mixer and use your hands to bring all the mixture together into a smooth ball of dough.

Wrap it in cling film and chill in the fridge for 30 minutes or more as this makes it much easier to roll.

Once it has chilled, put the ball of dough on a floured surface and roll it out to 0.5cm thick and cut into rounds.

Put the biscuits onto a couple of baking sheets lined with baking parchment and put in the oven for 15 minutes.

Let them cool for 5 minutes on the baking trays then sprinkle with caster sugar and transfer to a wire rack to cool completely.

When they have completely cooled, lay the biscuits between layers of baking parchment and transport in an airtight container. Serve them with a couple of stems of fresh lavender on the plate for the full fancy effect.

Prep time: 20 minutes,
Cooking time: 15 minutes
Makes: 12 to 16 biscuits

SMOKED TROUT, CELERIAC & BEETROOT SALAD

I love this dish. The earthiness of the beetroot and celeriac provide the base notes, while the delicate smokiness of the trout plays against the peppery tang of the watercress. The horseradish dressing adds a whack of heat. Smoked salmon or slices of smoked duck would work well too.

Ingredients

350g hot-smoked trout fillets

80g watercress

1 large handful of walnut or pecan halves

200g cooked beetroot

100g celeriac

1 tbsp lemon juice

An apple or pear

Dressing

3 tbsp crème fraîche

2 tsp horseradish sauce

Juice of ½ lemon

Salt and black pepper

A few small airtight tubs for transporting, a wide low dish to serve it in, a cutting board and a sharp knife for the apple or pear

Method

Flake the trout into bite-sized pieces and put them in a small sealable tub along with the watercress and the nuts.

Grate half the beetroot, cut the rest into slices and then quarters. Put the slices and grated beetroot in another container.

Peel the celeriac, grate half of it and cut the remaining half into slices, then into matchstick-sized pieces. Put them in a container, add the lemon juice and put the lid on the container.

Put the crème fraîche, the horseradish, salt and pepper and juice of half a lemon in a small, lidded pot. Shake vigorously to combine thoroughly.

Transport the tubs, dressing and apple in a cool box with a knife and a small board.

At the picnic, spread the watercress out on the dish, then add the trout and nuts across it. Scatter the beetroot and celeriac sticks on top and spoon little piles of the grated beetroot and celeriac around the edge. Slice the apple (or pear) thinly, cut into bite-sized pieces and add this to the salad. Finally spoon the dressing over the top.

Prep time: 20 minutes
Cooking time: none
Serves: 4 as a main dish

GROWN-UP SAUSAGE ROLL

The perennial picnic favourite has been given a grown-up makeover with some fennel and fresh apple. If you like a bit of spiciness, add quarter of a finely chopped, fresh red chilli. The finished dish is one large sausage roll that makes an impressive centrepiece, so transport it whole, if possible, or cut it into eight slices.

Ingredients

375g pre-rolled puff pastry

6 large, good-quality pork sausages

1 tsp fennel seeds

1 small apple, about 90g, grated

6 fresh sage leaves, finely shredded

1 small egg, beaten

1 tbsp sesame seeds

Mustard to serve

Method

Preheat the oven to 210°C/Fan 190°C/415°F/Gas mark 6.

Put an upturned baking tray or roasting tin on the middle shelf to provide a hot surface for the bottom of the sausage roll. Slit the sausage skins, put the meat into a bowl and discard the skins.

Toast the fennel seeds in a hot dry frying pan for a minute or two then crush them to release the aroma and flavours. Put the seeds into the bowl with the sausage meat, along with the grated apple. Use your hands to give it a good mix so it's well combined.

Unroll the pastry and scatter the shredded sage leaves across it. Form the sausage meat into a large sausage shape to fit the pastry and lay it on top. On either side of the meat cut the pastry into an equal number of diagonal slits, about 1.5cm apart.

Starting at the top on one side, bring the strips one by one, alternating from either side over the sausage meat to make a plait effect. Tuck the edges under the sausage meat and leave either end of the sausage exposed. Cut away any excess. Slide this onto a second, lined baking tray. Brush the top of the pastry with beaten egg and scatter the sesame seeds on the top.

Put the baking tray on top of the upturned baking tray in the oven and bake for 40 minutes until it has turned a golden colour. Immediately slide the sausage roll onto a wire rack to allow it to cool completely before packing for your picnic. Take a good mustard to serve with it.

Prep time: 30 minutes
Cooking time: 40 minutes
Serves: 6 to 8

ROSE MERINGUES
WITH RASPBERRY CREAM

A plate of these pretty, delicate rose pink meringues on my picnic rug has me momentarily believing I'm a fashionable lady in a scene from a period drama, picnicking with handsome cricket-playing chaps called Tarquin and Humphrey. You need an electric mixer, a piping bag and time to let them dry, but I promise the wow factor makes the effort worth it.

Ingredients

For the meringues

2 large eggs

1 tsp rosewater

150g caster sugar

Small pinch of salt

¼ tsp red gel food colouring

For the cream

50g raspberries

1 tbsp icing sugar

75ml double cream

For serving

100g fresh raspberries

Method

Preheat the oven to 140°C/275°F/Gas mark 1 and don't use the fan on the oven.

Separate the eggs and retain the whites. Put the egg whites into a very clean bowl and use an electric whisk on a fast setting to whisk the egg whites until they turn white and form stiff peaks.

With the whisk running, add the rosewater then the caster sugar, a tablespoon at a time, making sure it has been mixed in before adding the next. Add the food colouring (make sure you use the gel version) before the last few spoons of sugar.

When all the sugar has been added it should form stiff, satiny looking peaks. Spoon into a piping bag with a 1.5cm fluted nozzle and pipe the individual meringues (each about 5cm wide) onto a baking tray lined with parchment paper.

Bake in the oven for an hour. Turn the oven off without opening the door and leave for 4 hours, or preferably overnight.

On picnic day, make the cream by putting the raspberries in a sieve and use the back of a spoon to pulp them through it, collecting the thick juice in a bowl. Sift the icing sugar into the raspberry juice and mix well. Finally, add the double cream to the bowl and whip the cream until it turns into soft pretty pink peaks.

At the picnic, scatter the meringues and fresh raspberries on a serving platter with a bowl of pink cream in the middle. Then ask Tarquin to feed them to you.

Prep time: 30 minutes
Cooking time: 1 hour, plus resting time
Serves: 4, makes about 30

QUICK FIG & BLUE CHEESE
TARTLETS

Figs, honey and blue cheese make a great team on top of a tart. The fact that these smart little tarts can be packed and ready to go in 30 minutes makes them a fine choice for a stylish picnic. You could also scatter a few chopped walnuts over the top before serving, if you fancy.

Ingredients

3 figs, not too squashy

60g stilton or other good blue cheese

340g pack of pre-rolled puff pastry

1 tbsp runny honey

9cm pastry cutter

Method

Preheat the oven to 210°C/Fan 190°C/410°F/Gas mark 6.

Using the pastry cutter, cut eight rounds of pastry and lay them onto two baking trays lined with baking parchment.

Use a knife to score a circle around the edge of each pastry circle, about 0.5cm from the edge.

Cut the figs into thin slices and arrange them onto the pastry rounds, keeping them within the inner scored circle.

Crumble the blue cheese, and distribute it equally between the tarts.

Drizzle a little honey on the top of each tartlet and put them in the oven for 15 minutes, until the pastry has puffed up around the edges and the cheese has begun to melt.

Slide onto a wire rack to cool then pack in an airtight container.

Prep time: 10 minutes
Cooking time: 15 minutes
Makes: 8 tartlets

HERBY NEW POTATO & BROAD BEAN SALAD

Small bites are more refined, so my mum tells me. With that in mind, try to get the potatoes all of a similar, small size, as it does make a difference to how the dish looks. This is also the reason for taking the cooked broad beans out of their skins as they are such a lovely bright green colour without their grey coats and they taste fresher.

Ingredients

500g baby new potatoes

300g broad beans

1 heaped tbsp coriander, chopped

1 tsp chives, chopped finely

1 tsp mint, chopped finely

1 tsp rosemary, chopped finely

1 thin slice of red onion, diced very finely (optional)

2 heaped tsp capers

Large handful of rocket leaves

Dressing

1 tsp lemon juice and a large pinch of unwaxed lemon zest

3 tbsp good olive oil or rapeseed oil

1 tbsp cider vinegar

Large pinch of sea salt flakes

Method

Boil the potatoes in salted water for about 15 minutes or until tender, then drain them. Run them under cold water and leave them to drain again.

Put the broad beans into a pan of fresh boiling water for 2 to 3 minutes. Drain immediately and run cold water over them. Squeeze each of them at one end to pop them out of their skins and discard the skins.

Put the dressing ingredients together in a jam jar and shake it vigorously.

Put the beans in a bowl with the potatoes and pour the dressing over them. Add the chopped herbs, red onion (if using) and the capers, and toss to combine everything.

Put the salad in a sealable container to take to your picnic. Take the rocket in a separate bag and add to the potatoes before serving.

Try adding four hard-boiled quail eggs, cut in half, or edamame beans

Prep time: 15 minutes
Cooking time: 15 minutes
Serves: 4

ELDERFLOWER & RASPBERRY
VICTORIA SPONGE

All the best picnic rugs need a proper sponge cake. This is a recipe from my good friend Emma. She travels the world as a BA cabin crew member but, when she comes home, spends hours baking cakes to wind down and feel homely again. All of her cakes are fabulous, but this is my favourite.

Ingredients

Sponge

230g unsalted butter or margarine

200g caster sugar

2 tbsp elderflower cordial

4 medium eggs

230g self-raising flower

1 tsp baking power

2 x 20cm sandwich tins, lightly greased and lined

Filling and decoration

4 heaped tsp full fat cream cheese

8 tsp elderflower cordial

400g icing sugar

250g raspberries

Edible flowers such as pansies, borage, nasturtiums or camellias, or use the pretty ready-made icing flowers from the shops

Method

Preheat the oven to 190°C/Fan 170°C/375°F/Gas mark 5.

Melt the butter and pour into a mixing bowl. Either using a manual or electric hand mixer, whisk in the caster sugar and the elderflower cordial for at least a minute.

Add the eggs and whisk again until they are combined (the mixture will initially separate). Sieve the flour and baking power into the mixture then, using a spatula, fold the mixture until it is all combined.

Evenly distribute the mixture between the two prepared tins and place into the middle of the oven for about 20 minutes until the cakes are risen, golden in colour and springy to the touch.

Leave to cool, then take out of the tins.

For the filling, thoroughly mix the cream cheese and cordial together. Sieve the icing sugar in gradually and mix until smooth.

Place one of the sponges on a plate, flat side up. Smooth about two-thirds of the filling evenly over the flat side of this sponge. Loosely mash the raspberries in a bowl and spread these over the creamed filling, then add the other cake on top.

Evenly cover the top of the cake with the remaining third of the filling and arrange the edible or sugar flowers on top.

Prep time: 25 minutes
Cooking time: 20 minutes
Serves: 6

FETA, COURGETTE, PEA & MINT FRITTATA

Frittata is such a versatile dish. It can be customised in any way you fancy, or in any way the contents of your fridge allows. This one has a fresh vibe with the mint and courgettes, and a little fresh chilli to spice things up. I make this in a loaf tin, using a cake liner for easy baking, then it can be cut and packed in finger slices.

Ingredients

1 large courgette

A handful of fresh mint leaves, roughly chopped

1 small red onion, chopped finely

¼ fresh red chilli, finely sliced, with some for decoration

8 medium eggs

100g frozen peas

4 spring onions, sliced

60g feta or hard goat's cheese

Salt and black pepper

23cm x 12cm (2lb) loaf tin

Method

Preheat the oven to 190°C/Fan 170°C/375°F/Gas mark 5.

Prepare a loaf tin with a cake liner or line with baking parchment.

Lay a piece of kitchen paper on a chopping board and grate the courgettes onto it. Using another piece of kitchen paper, push down on the courgette to soak up a little of the excess moisture.

Put the mint leaves into a bowl with the grated courgette. Add the chopped red onion and the red chilli.

Heat a little oil in a large frying pan and fry the courgette and onion mix for about 5 minutes until the onions start to soften.

Meanwhile, beat the eggs in a bowl and season well with salt and pepper. Pour the fried courgette mixture into the bowl of beaten eggs, add the peas and spring onions, and gently mix. Crumble in three-quarters of the cheese.

Pour the egg mixture into the lined loaf tin and crumble the last bit of cheese over the top. Place a few slices of red chilli and some mint leaves on the top too.

Put in the oven and bake for 25 minutes until set. Check that the centre is cooked, if not leave for another 5 minutes.

When it has completely cooled, slice into 8 fingers and pack between greaseproof paper.

Prep time: 15 minutes
Cooking time: 25 minutes
Makes: 8 generous slices

GORGEOUSLY REFRESHING
GAZPACHO

Cool gazpacho on a hot summer's day, with its simple Mediterranean flavours of ripe tomato, garlic, olive oil and red onions, is a truly wonderful thing. Serve the soup in china tea cups to feel extra posh.

Ingredients

1½ slices stale white bread

1 large garlic clove, crushed and chopped

750g ripe, vine-ripened tomatoes

½ small red onion, finely chopped

½ cucumber, peeled and chopped into small pieces

2 spring onions, topped, tailed and sliced finely

1 medium red pepper, deseeded and chopped into small pieces

½ orange or yellow pepper, deseeded and chopped into small pieces

½ tsp salt

15ml balsamic vinegar

1 tsp sugar

75ml extra-virgin olive oil

A handful of basil leaves

Method

Tear the bread up and put it in a small bowl with the garlic. Pour just enough water to cover the bread and put it to one side.

Put the tomatoes in a heatproof bowl and pour on enough boiling water to cover them. Leave them for about 3 minutes and the skins will split. Scoop them out and put to one side until they are cool enough for you to peel. Discard the skins.

Balance a sieve over a clean bowl. Chop the tomatoes in half, scoop out the seeds and put the seeds in the sieve so that the juices drip into the bowl.

Chop the tomato flesh into small pieces and put in a bowl. Add in the red onion, cucumber, spring onions, peppers, salt, vinegar, sugar and olive oil.

Squeeze the water out of the bread, then put the bread and the garlic into the bowl with the tomatoes and the other ingredients.

Use the back of a spoon to push the remaining juice out of the tomato seeds through the sieve then pour the captured juice into the bowl. Discard the seeds. Use a hand blender or food processor to blend everything together for a couple of minutes.

Put the soup in the fridge to chill for at least 3 hours, then decant into flasks or insulated cups to keep it as cold as possible.

Serve with freshly torn basil leaves on the top.

Prep time: 20 minutes
Cooking time: 3 hours to chill
Serves: 4

PORK & APRICOT
LATTICE PIE

A latticed pork pie is a must for any formal picnic. This recipe looks immense, but it genuinely doesn't take that long to make. All the raw filling ingredients are combined in one bowl and the hot water pastry is quick and simple to make. The only lengthy bit is the time in the oven. Worth the wait I'd say.

Ingredients

Filling

200g pork shoulder steak, fat cut off

200g pork mince (5% fat)

1 small onion, peeled and finely chopped

50g dried apricots, chopped into small pieces

Large pinch of ground nutmeg

1 tsp sea salt

1 heaped tsp fresh rosemary leaves, finely chopped

18cm loose bottom, round pie or cake tin ➤→

Method

Prepare the filling by cutting the shoulder steak into small pieces, no bigger than 1cm square. Put this into a mixing bowl with the pork mince, the onion, apricots, nutmeg and rosemary. Use your hands to combine this thoroughly.

To make the pastry, sift the flours and salt into a large mixing bowl. Add the chilled butter and use your fingers to rub it in until the mixture resembles breadcrumbs.

Melt the lard in a saucepan, take off the heat and leave for a couple of minutes.

Add the salt to 130ml of boiling water and pour this onto the lard.

Make a well in the flour and pour the boiling water and lard mixture into it, mixing with a fork as you pour.

Keep mixing until all of the flour is combined then use your hands to bring it all together as a dough. Give it a bit of a knead, it will be a bit stretchy, but that is fine.

Let the pastry cool a little then roll it out into a large circle (about 0.5cm thick). Make sure the circle is bigger than the pie tin, with enough pastry to come all the way up the sides too.

Place it over the tin and use your hands to gently push the dough out to cover the base and sides of the tin in a thin but even layer of pastry. Make sure there are no cracks or holes. ➤→

Prep time: 35 minutes
Cooking time: 1 hour 20 minutes
Serves: 6

PORK & APRICOT
LATTICE PIE

Pastry

200g plain flour

140g strong white flour

½ tsp salt

70g lard or Trex

50g butter, chilled and cubed

130ml boiling water

1 small egg, beaten

There will be an overhang so, using a sharp knife, cut the excess pastry off, making sure to leave it about 1cm longer than the actual tin to allow for shrinkage in the oven.

Bring the excess pastry together into a ball and roll it out into a rectangle, about 0.5cm thick. This will make the lattice topping. Cut the pastry into 1.5cm strips and put to one side.

Add the filling to the pie, pushing it down firmly into the tin so that it is tightly packed.

To make the lattice effect, lay pastry strips vertically across the pie. Next, fold every other strip back on itself. You are bending it in half. Lay a strip of pastry, horizontally on the filling across the middle. It will lie across the strips that haven't been bent backwards. Now fold the bent strips back in place so they lie over the horizontal one.

Repeat this method, alternating the strips that you bend backwards to achieve a weave effect.

Preheat the oven to 210°C/Fan 190°C/410°F/Gas mark 6 and place an upturned baking tray in it. This helps to cook the bottom of the pie.

Brush the top of the lattice pie with the beaten egg and place the pie on a baking tray. Put this in the oven on top of the upturned tray.

Bake for 1 hour and 20 minutes.

Take the pie out of the oven and, holding it firmly, gently tip the tin sideways to pour away the excess liquid fat. Take the pie out of the tin and leave it to cool on a wire rack, ready to pack.

MENU IDEAS

1 **Scarlet salmon** | **French bean and pea salad** | **Jewelled cous cous salad** | **Quick fig and blue cheese tartlets** | **Coronation chicken salad** | **Lemon and ginger cheesecake bites** | **Boozy berry picnic puddings** | **Mango Bellinis**

A picnic for the ultimate evening do. Take the candelabra, then china and the kitchen sink. These occasions make carrying all that kit worth it.

2 **Pork and apricot lattice pie** | **Pickled cucumbers** | **Potato salad** | **Elderflower and raspberry Victoria sponge** | **Spicy scotch egg** | **Sophisticated shortbread** | **Elderflower Collins**

For a gathering on a country-house lawn, think scenes from a period drama and unashamedly traditional picnic fare.

3 **Gazpacho** | **Scarlet salmon** | **Peach, tomato and mozzarella salad** | **New potato and broad bean salad** | **Rose meringues** | **Boozy fruit jellies**

A fine, delicate dining spread to impress the in-laws.

4 **Tropical picnic ham** | **Smoked trout salad** | **Grown-up sausage roll** | **Pickled cucumbers** | **Sunny salad** | **Potato salad** | **Boozy berry picnic puddings** | **Orange zest brownies**

A celebration luncheon. Some moments in life deserve marking in the best way possible – good people, great food and beautiful landscapes.

MARVELLOUS PLACES
FOR THE
PERFECT POSH PICNIC

—— CHATSWORTH ESTATE ——

DERBYSHIRE

Taking your hamper to Chatsworth will guarantee a posh picnic. It is perhaps England's finest house and estate. The opulence displayed in the 126 rooms, dripping with Old Master paintings and lavish furnishings, continues outside in the 105-acre garden. The gardens have been attentively refined over six centuries, offering a wealth of options as a place to fine dine from your hamper. The manicured lawns in front of the house with a view of the house, bridge and fountain is a classic choice, or you could pick a spot down on the riverbank – the views are just as impressive. Then there are the rose gardens, kitchen gardens, under the gaze of a classical sculpture, or next to the 300-year-old cascade water feature and enormous Emperor Fountain – all of which will just add to the grandeur of your experience.

FIND IT There is an entrance fee to the Chatworth Estate. If you are using a sat nav use the postcode DE45 1PN.

—— SOUTH LAWN ——

POLESDEN LACEY, SURREY

The South Lawn, known as Lady Greville's Lawn, is an exquisite place to set up your rug of refined refreshments. A sense of high society pervades this place. The grand Edwardian house that opens out on to the lawns was the ultimate party house in the early 1900s. Society hostess Lady Maggie Greville bought and redesigned the house as a weekend retreat from her Mayfair home and it became a place to throw open the doors to the great, the good and the well connected. The future George VI and Queen Elizabeth, the Queen Mother, honeymooned at Polesden Lacey, King Edward VII attended parties here, as did Winston Churchill. Now you and your guests can add to the list by partaking in a bit of fine dining out on the lawn.

With the house behind you, the majestic vista of the ancient Surrey woodland is as impressive in autumn as it is in the summer.

FIND IT Great Bookham, near Dorking, Surrey, RH5 6BD. Note there is an entrance fee, free to National Trust members. Don't miss the brown sign as you enter the village of Great Bookham, indicating the turn up to Polesden Lacey.

—— LILY HILL PARK ——

BRACKNELL, BERKSHIRE

Enjoy a little taste of Victoriana in Lily Hill Park. This gorgeous space, close to the centre of Bracknell, encompasses 56 acres of restored heritage parkland and formal gardens, free for public use. Lily Hill House, at the head of the park, was built in 1814 on the site of an old hunting lodge, when Windsor Forest extended this far. After many owners, it has now been turned into office space but the gardens and grounds have been lovingly restored, maintained and developed, much of it by local community groups. There are some beautiful areas to hold a grand outdoor occasion. There's a wildflower meadow, an orchard planted with Victorian varieties of apples, and parkland with ornamental trees, an Edwardian water garden and an ancient woodland. However, I suggest you head for England's longest picnic table (60ft long). It's carved from a single piece of wood, once the trunk of a Lows Fir that was felled by a storm.

FIND IT Lily Hill is free. It is located just east of Bracknell town centre, north of A329 London Road. There are 10 pedestrian access points around the park, linking to London Road, Lily Hill Drive and Lily Hill Road. Free car parking is available in two council-owned car parks close to the park. Postcode for Lily Hill car park is RG12 2RX, and Lily Hill Drive car park RG12 2UG.

—— FOUNTAINS ABBEY ——

NORTH YORKSHIRE

There must be a reason why Fountains Abbey appears on so many best picnic spots surveys. The 12th-century Cistercian monks who built the abbey certainly picked a good spot. Visit and you'll see why. It really is a special treat to feast with friends on the abbey green. The place oozes atmosphere. The accompanying Studley Water Gardens with its lakes and follies just adds to the splendour of the surroundings. There's a medieval royal deer park on the banks of the River Skell to explore and a play park for the younger members of the picnic party.

FIND IT There is an entrance fee, free to National Trust members. It is 12 miles north of Harrogate and well signposted off the B6265 south west of Ripon. Nearest postcode is HG4 3DY.

SHERINGHAM PARK

nr CROMER, NORFOLK

Enjoy the results of the landscaping genius Humphry (without an e) Repton. In the mid-1800s, he designed more than 400 grand gardens including Longleat (Wiltshire), Woburn Abbey (Bedfordshire) and Russell Square (London). Sheringham Park is a fine example of his work, incorporating his signature style of rolling parkland, flower gardens, conservatories and formal terraces. Owned by the National Trust, it is free and open to the public to enjoy. Positioned on the north Norfolk coast, the sea views are breathtaking, so pick a coastal spot for your hamper. With nearly a thousand acres of parkland to explore, there are many private glades to picnic in too. May and June are particularly good months to visit when all the rhododendrons and azaleas are displaying their full floral beauty.

FIND IT Main entrance at junction A148/B1157 Upper Sheringham, Norfolk, NR26 8TL, 5 miles west of Cromer, 6 miles east of Holt. Parking is available.

WOLLATON PARK

NOTTINGHAM

This is a stunner of a venue for a fine feast. Based around a spectacular Grade I listed Elizabethan mansion, Wollaton Hall, the parkland stretches to 500 acres of formal gardens, ornamental lake and boathouse, avenues of ancient trees, and it is particularly well known for its herds of free roaming red and fallow deer. Best of all, it's free to come and roam here yourself. The hall is now the city's Natural History Museum, which is also free to enter.

The grounds host annual music festivals, summer seasons of outdoor theatre and cinema, sporting and orienteering events and lots more so there are many reasons to create a fine banquet. Or just pick a sunny day and enjoy the splendour for the sake of it.

FIND IT Wollaton Park, Wollaton, Nottinghamshire, NG8 2AE. There are car parks and toilets on site.

— MARGAM COUNTRY PARK —

SOUH WALES

Margam Country Park surrounds the Grade I Margam Castle, which is actually a 19th-century Tudor Gothic mansion. The 850-acre country estate is situated two miles east of Port Talbot on the southern slopes of Mynydd Margam. The house is one of many reincarnations of the original building on this historical site, once a 12th-century Norman abbey.

For just the parking fee, visitors are free to wander and lay out a picnic rug in a perfect setting. You'll be surrounded by beautiful trees, shrubs and flowers, lakes and long vistas that have been enjoyed since medieval times. The park is a haven for bird life, in particular skylarks, buzzards, kestrels and sparrow hawks, as well as swans, geese and kingfishers around the lake and streams. For a little haven of peace, head to the Japanese Garden.

FIND IT Margam Country Park, Abbey Road, Margam, SA13 2TJ.

— OXFORD BOTANTIC GARDEN — AND ARBORETUM

OXFORD

For a serene and refined spot, you would do well to choose the walled gardens here. Dating from 1621, it is the oldest section in what is England's oldest botanic garden. For a reasonable entrance fee, you and your picnic guests can indulge in the beauty of this oasis. There are 6,000 different types of plant across herbaceous borders and glass houses. Picnics are positively encouraged and there are plenty of benches. In the walled garden, you'll find the geographic beds that display year-round plants and flowers from South Africa, Japan and South America. The lower garden is adjacent to Christ Church Meadow and bordered by the River Cherwell, and provides a tranquil space, perfect for picnics. In the far left hand corner sits a bench that has become a place of pilgrimage for many visitors to the Garden. It is a significant location in Philip Pullman's 'His Dark Materials' trilogy, where characters Will and Lyra can meet between their respective worlds.

FIND IT Oxford Botanic Garden, Rose Lane, Oxford, OX1 4AZ. Park in the public car park on St Clements Street, OX4 1AB. The gardens are a 5-minute walk. Drop someone off with the hamper at the entrance while you park.

ABBEY GARDENS

BURY ST EDMUNDS, SUFFOLK

Lay your banquet-in-a-hamper out among the floral displays. The Abbey Gardens are a colourful gem in the heart of historic Bury St Edmunds. The Abbleby Rose Garden has more than 400 rose bushes and is named after John Abbleby, one of the many American servicemen who were stationed here during World War II. The bench in this part of the garden is made from a wing of an American bomber. Alternatively, the water garden is a tranquil spot if you are looking for some shade on a hot summer day.

As well as the Abbey, which is free to enter, the ruins of an 11th-century Benedictine monastery are within the gardens. Once a site of pilgrimage, it's now a haven for picnickers who get to enjoy the serenity and beauty of these gardens with the grandeur of the Abbey as a back drop.

FIND IT Angel Hill, Bury St Edmunds, Suffolk, IP33 1LS. There is a charged car park opposite the Abbey Gate. Enter via the Abbey Gate entrance into the gardens on Angel Hill or via their Mustow Street entrance.

PORTMEIRION

PORTHMADOG, GWYNEDD, WALES

If you are putting on a spread for a special occasion, then this candy-coloured, Italian-style village, placed rather incongruously on a Welsh estuary, is a spectacular spot. There are more than 30 picnic tables and chairs dotted around, so pick a spot, any spot, and you'll be guaranteed a memorable setting. The magical village is the realisation of a life-long dream of architect Clough Williams-Ellis. There are 70 acres of subtropical forest trails, palm trees, lakes, the beach is pristine, and there are little coves to explore. But for once, it is the architecture itself that will hold your attention: the Italianate fountains, the pantheon, Mediterranean piazza, loggias, grand porticoes and brightly painted terracotta roofed houses definitely steal the limelight. And yes, it's where *The Prisoner* was filmed.

FIND IT Minffordd, Penrhyndeudraeth, Gwynedd, LL48 6ER. There is an entry charge. There is lots of parking close to the village centre.

6
BARBECUES

FOR GRILLS, GRIDDLES AND FOOD AROUND THE FIRE

Having a barbecue ignites a sense of excitement. Maybe it's our eternal fascination with fire and flame, or perhaps it's because food genuinely does seem to taste better when cooked and eaten outside. Cooking outside on a summer's day or balmy evening can be a real joy, even for those who usually avoid the kitchen.

These recipes suit all kinds of occasions: a fish supper on the beach, a simple lamb pasta dish cooked before sleeping under the stars and a vegetarian mushroom and chickpea burger to provide sustenance after a long country ramble.

Many portable barbecues on the market are cheap and lightweight, making the possibilities of being truly mobile a genuine option these days. However, the rules of barbecuing in public spaces varies: some councils and the Forestry Commission provide designated barbecuing areas, others ban them to avoid the land and property being scorched. If you are unsure, check in advance.

There are suggestions at the end of the chapter for really great places to fire up a barbecue around the country. Some of them have static public barbecues or fire pits that are free to turn up and use, others can be pre-booked and cost a fee in order to guarantee your place at the flame. Others have designated barbecue areas with tables and stands or pads to put your own barbecue on in order not to damage the grass.

One final note... Please never use disposable barbecues. They are drenched with chemicals that imbue your food with a terrible flavour and goodness knows what else. They can't be recycled and too many people throw them into public bins while still hot, causing fires. I don't recommend them!

MACKEREL WITH RHUBARB & SALSA

Beach picnics are the best as far as I'm concerned. Nothing beats fresh fish on the barbecue as the sun sets on a great day at the beach. Oily fish like mackerel cope with strong flavours like the mustard and rhubarb here, and I've added a cucumber mint salsa to add a ting of freshness.

Ingredients

6 whole mackerel, heads off and gutted (ask your fishmonger to do it for you)

5 tsp English mustard

10 sticks rhubarb, the pinker the better, chopped into 2cm pieces

Some oil spray for the barbecue

Salsa

1 cucumber, cut lengthways, deseeded and cut into small cubes

3 sprigs of fresh mint, leaves finely chopped

Splash of white wine vinegar

Method

Before the picnic Rinse the mackerel inside and out then pat dry with kitchen paper. Place each fish on a board and use a sharp knife to cut diagonal slashes 2cm apart on the flesh on both sides of the fish, but don't cut all the way through.

Rub the mustard across the flesh, making sure it goes down into the slashes, then put the fish in a strong, sealable freezer bag and store in a cool box to transport.

Put the chopped rhubarb in a separate, sealable freezer bag.

To make the salsa, put the cucumber in a tub with a lid, add the mint leaves and vinegar, and mix together.

At the picnic Heat your barbecue and spray it with a little oil. Put two squares of foil (about the size of a magazine) one on top of the other to make a double thickness. In the centre, put the rhubarb and add a splash of water (or wine). Fold the foil over to make a flat parcel, sealing it around the edges. When the barbecue is hot, place the mackerel and parcel of rhubarb on the grill. The mackerel will take about 5 minutes on each side. Turn them carefully so that the flesh doesn't fall apart.

After about 3 minutes take the rhubarb off the heat and check it has softened. Fold the foil open to make a little dish with the rhubarb in the middle. Once the mackerel has cooked, serve it alongside the rhubarb and cucumber salsa.

Cut a potato in half and rub it on the grill before heating to stop the fish from sticking

Prep time: 30 minutes
Cooking time: 10 minutes
Serves: 6

PIÑA
GRILLADA

The natural sugars in fresh fruit caramelise beautifully when they come into contact with a hot barbecue grill, transforming fruits such as pineapples, peaches and plums into utterly delicious desserts in an instant. This is a grown-up dessert because of the rum in the cream, but just leave out the booze for a younger crowd.

Ingredients

2 fresh pineapples, peeled, cored and cut into 12 rings

130g soft light brown sugar

3 heaped tsp cinnamon

100ml coconut milk

75ml double cream

2 tbsp rum

3 heaped tsp desiccated coconut (optional)

Method

Before the picnic Pack the pineapple rings in a sealed tub for transporting.

Combine the sugar and cinnamon in a separate tub with a lid.

Put the double cream in a bowl with the rum, if using, and use an electric hand whisk to whip it into soft peaks and decant into a bowl with a lid. Alternatively, you can mix the rum with some clotted cream when you get there.

Pack the coconut milk and a bowl for when you get to the picnic.

At the picnic Heat up the barbecue, and pour the coconut milk into a bowl.

Dip a pineapple ring into the coconut milk, then sprinkle each side with the sugar and cinnamon mixture and put it on to the heated barbecue. Repeat with all the other pineapple rings.

Cook the pineapple rings for about 4 minutes on each side until they start to soften and caramelise on the edges.

Take them off the heat and sprinkle the desiccated coconut over the top (if using). Serve with dollops of the rum cream.

Prep time: 10 minutes
Cooking time: 8 minutes
Serves: 6

_ HALLOUMI, WATERMELON _ & BULGUR WHEAT SALAD

This is a summery as it gets. Cooling mint, watermelon and cucumber contrast brilliantly with sticky and salty griddled halloumi. I've also fired things up a bit with a chilli coating on the halloumi, but if you don't want the spice, leave the chilli out and you'll have a sticky, herby coating that caramelises on the barbecue instead.

Ingredients

600g halloumi

3 tbsp sweet chilli sauce

3 tbsp fresh coriander leaves, chopped

2 tbsp honey

2 garlic cloves, minced

Juice of 1 large lemon

400g bulgur wheat

4 spring onions, sliced

A couple of handfuls of toasted almonds

2 sprigs mint leaves, shredded

Handful of flat-leafed parsley, roughly chopped

500g watermelon, cut into the size of Dairylea triangles

1 cucumber, cut into bite-sized, angular shapes

2 tbsp olive oil

Method

Before the picnic Cut the halloumi into 2cm thick slices. Slice the block so you have wide squares rather than narrow rectangles from the side.

In a plastic tub, mix the chilli sauce, coriander leaves, honey, garlic and two tablespoons of lemon juice. Put the halloumi slices into the sauce and coat both sides of the cheese. Leave in the tub with the lid on and chill until you're ready to cook.

Cook the bulgur wheat according the packet instructions. Drain and leave to cool. Mix the spring onions, almonds, mint and parsley into the cooled bulgur wheat. Mix the remaining lemon juice with the oil and mix this through the bulgur wheat too. Put it in a tub with a lid.

Slice the skin off the watermelon triangles, put them in a tub and add the chopped cucumber. Seal and keep cool.

At the picnic Oil the barbecue and get it hot. Grill the pieces of cheese for a couple of minutes each until they have started to pick up lovely brown grill marks across them.

Meanwhile, tip the remaining sauce from the halloumi tub onto the bulgur wheat and mix through, adding the watermelon and cucumber, and tip it all out onto a serving platter.

Take the cheese off the grill and cut the squares diagonally so the halloumi is about the same size as the watermelon slices. Place the grilled halloumi over the salad and serve immediately.

Prep time: 25 minutes
Cooking time: 6 minutes
Serves: 6

MARMALADE CHICKEN
WITH SWEET POTATO WEDGES

We've all got half-used jars of jams, chutneys and other preserves in the back of the fridge. It's such a wasted resource as they are the perfect extra ingredient to jazz up a recipe. Here I'm making the most of marmalade as a coating for chicken thighs. Serve it with some sweet potato wedges for a great value crowd pleaser.

Ingredients

2 large sweet potatoes, (about 900g) washed, skins left on and cut into wedges

8 chicken thighs (or drumsticks), skin on

4 tbsp rapeseed oil

1 heaped tsp Chinese five spice

3 heaped tbsp marmalade

2 garlic cloves, minced

½ red chilli, deseeded and finely chopped

Salt and black pepper

Method

Before the picnic Parboil the sweet potato wedges for about 5 to 6 minutes. Drain and pat them dry with a piece of kitchen paper then drizzle with a little oil, salt and pepper and leave to cool – ideally spread out on a tray or large plate. When they have cooled, pack in an airtight container for taking on the picnic.

Put the chicken thighs in a large freezer bag. Mix half a teaspoon of Chinese five spice with a tablespoon of rapeseed oil and add this to the bag. Squish it around to coat the chicken and store in a cool box to transport.

For the coating, mix the marmalade, two tablespoons of oil, garlic, chilli and the other half a teaspoon of the Chinese five spice in a tub with a lid. Seal tightly and pack for transporting.

At the picnic Brush a little oil on the griddle and get your barbecue hot. Place the chicken thighs on the grill and cook for about 20 to 25 minutes, turning frequently. Take the pieces off the heat and coat them with the marmalade mixture, making sure they are completely covered, and put back on the grill.

Put the sweet potato wedges on at this point. They will take about 5 to 10 minutes to start crisping up.

Cook the chicken for another 10 minutes, again turning frequently as the sugar in the marmalade will burn a little.

Once the chicken is cooked, serve them with the wedges and plenty of napkins.

Prep time: 25 minutes
Cooking time: 35 minutes
Serves: 4

MEDITERRANEAN LAMB PASTA

A hearty family meal of pasta, veggies and delicious barbecued meat. It can all be prepped at home, so you only need to take charge of the grill. If you want to get ahead, roast the veggies at home instead of barbecuing them. Let them cool then wrap them, along with the juices, in a foil parcel that you can pop on the grill to heat up when cooking the lamb.

Ingredients

1 aubergine, cut into 1cm round slices

1 large courgette, cut into thin slices, lengthways

1 red and 1 yellow pepper, tops cut off, deseeded, cut into 2cm wide slices, lengthways

1 red onion, peeled and cut into thin wedges

3 large garlic cloves

4 tbsp rapeseed or olive oil

500g rigatoni pasta

100g toasted pine nuts

Fresh basil leaves (about 8)

Fresh mint leaves (about 8)

700g lamb loin steaks

Zest and juice of ½ unwaxed lemon

2 large sprigs of fresh rosemary

Salt and black pepper

Two large handfuls of baby spinach leaves

Method

Before the picnic Put all the prepared vegetables in a sealable freezer bag and add two tablespoons of oil and two crushed garlic cloves. Store in the cool bag.

Cook the pasta according to instructions, then drain immediately and rinse under cold water. Drizzle a tablespoon of oil over the pasta and mix through to stop it sticking together. When it is completely cool, put the pasta into a plastic container, add the pine nuts, mint and basil leaves and put the lid on.

Mix the last clove of garlic with the zest and juice of half a lemon and a tablespoon of olive oil, then put into a second freezer bag. Bash the fresh rosemary with a rolling pin, rub this all over the lamb, then season it with salt and pepper. Put the lamb and rosemary sprigs into the bag and massage it around so the lamb is fully coated. Store in a cool box until needed.

At the picnic Oil the grill and get it up to heat. Spread the vegetables in a single layer across the barbecue and cook them until they soften and begin to char a little. Take them off the grill and wrap in foil.

Add the lamb to the grill. Sear it and turn it until it has browned all over. Continue to cook to your liking: 3 to 4 minutes on each side for medium rare, 5 minutes on each side for medium.

Take the lamb off the heat, wrap in foil and rest it for 5 minutes. Slice it thickly. Put the pasta in a bowl with the veggies, the baby spinach and the lamb. Gently toss and serve immediately.

Prep time: 30 minutes
Cooking time: 10 minutes
Serves: 6

CHICKEN SATAY
SKEWERS

This recipe adds some serious charm to a piece of chicken. It's a gorgeous, gooey chicken satay recipe that sings with all the glory of sweet and savoury. And best of all, you'll find most of the ingredients in your cupboard. You might just need to add the tin of coconut milk.

Ingredients

6 chicken breasts, cut diagonally into long strips about 2cm wide

Juice of 2 limes, zest of 1

2½ tbsp soy sauce

3 tbsp runny honey

4 tbsp peanut butter

1½ heaped tsp mild curry powder

2 large garlic cloves, very finely chopped or grated

8 tbsp coconut milk

12 metal skewers

Large, plastic tub with a lid that will fit the chicken on the skewers

Method

Before the picnic In a bowl, put the zest and juice of the limes, soy sauce, honey, peanut butter, curry powder and garlic. Mix them together really well. It might look a bit strange at first as the peanut butter separates with the lime, but keep mixing and it will turn into a lovely paste.

Thread the chicken pieces onto the skewers and lay them into the tub. Take a third (not all) of the marinade and thoroughly cover the chicken pieces in it. Put the lid on and put in the fridge until ready to transport. If you don't have a big enough tub, you can put the skewers into a large sealable freezer bag and squidge the chicken around in the bag so that it is thoroughly coated.

Put the rest of the marinade in a small saucepan on a low heat, add the coconut milk and heat it gently, stirring constantly. When it is hot and blended together, take it off the heat and put to one side until it is cool enough to put into a tub or jar for transporting.

At the picnic Wipe the grill with oil before heating it. Once it's nice and hot, put the skewers on the grill and keep watching them while they cook, turning them frequently. They will take around 4 or 5 minutes on each side, but cut into the chicken to check if in doubt. Put the cooked chicken skewers on a plate and pour the coconut satay sauce over the top to serve.

Prep time: 25 minutes
Cooking time: 15 minutes
Serves: 6

MUSHROOM BURGERS

A great vegetarian option, this recipe uses big portobello mushrooms. I've called them burgers because the mushrooms become the buns and so look like burgers. You can fill them with different cheeses and flavours – this version uses stilton. The stuffing is made from chickpeas and nuts, though grated breadcrumbs work well as a stuffing base too.

Ingredients

12 large portobello mushrooms, wiped not washed, and don't peel the caps

Olive oil

2 x 400g tin chickpeas

Juice and zest of 1 unwaxed lemon

4 spring onions, thinly sliced

1 garlic clove, grated

A good pinch of fresh thyme leaves

100g walnut halves

100g pecan halves

250g stilton, crumbled

3 tbsp fruit-based chutney, such as pear, apple or cranberry

Salt and black pepper

Method

Before the picnic Pour a little olive oil into your hand and hold one mushroom upside down with the other hand to soak the top of the mushroom in the oil. Pinch the stalk out then put the cap upside down on a plate and repeat with the other mushrooms.

Drain and rinse the chickpeas, pour them into a bowl and, using a fork or a masher, roughly mash the chickpeas. Add the lemon juice, zest, spring onions, garlic, thyme, nuts, chutney and the stilton. Season well then use your hands to mix it thoroughly.

Divide the stuffing into six and make into flat patties by squeezing the ingredients together. The patties will be a bit loose.

Put one stuffing pattie on each of the six mushrooms and then pop the empty mushrooms on top to create a burger effect. Press them together but not too hard that you split them. Don't worry about the fact the mushroom burgers look really tall, they will cook down to half the height.

Store them in a sealed, lidded container until you are ready to use them. Make sure the mushrooms are packed in tightly so that the stuffing doesn't come out in transit.

At the picnic Oil the barbecue griddle, heat to a medium heat and place the mushrooms on it. They will take about 8 to 10 minutes on each side to cook but keep an eye on them. The mushrooms will reduce in size, and can be cut in half or into wedges like a small pie to serve.

Prep time: 25 minutes
Cooking time: 20 minutes
Serves: 6

SUNNY SALAD

It's bright orange, sweet and a bit nutty. This happy-looking salad adds a pizzazz to any picnic. A versatile side dish, it can work well with cold meats like the tropical ham and is great with fish, such as the cured salmon or grilled mackerel. The added bonus is that it's healthy and nutritious, so you can offset all of those indulgent desserts in your hamper.

Ingredients

100g cashew nuts,
or unsalted peanuts

½ tsp cumin seeds

2 large oranges

4 radishes

5 large carrots, as young
and fresh as possible

Salt and black pepper

Dressing

1 tbsp rapeseed or olive oil

1 tsp cider vinegar, balsamic or
red wine vinegar

½ tsp poppy or sesame seeds
(optional)

A drizzle of honey

Method

Toast the cashew nuts in a dry frying pan. Use a medium-high heat and stay with the pan (I've burnt too many nuts by wandering off).

Shake or stir the frying pan to keep the nuts moving. It will take about 5 to 6 minutes before they start to toast and turn brown. Once you notice the first one browning, add the cumin seeds for the last couple of minutes to toast these too.

Tip them out onto a plate to cool.

Peel and cut off all the skin and white pith from the oranges. Then cut the segments out from between the membranes. This is a little fiddly, but worth it for the results. Do this over a bowl or a plate where you can catch all the juice.

Cut the segments in half and put into the container you will transport your salad in.

Slice the radishes into very fine rounds and add this to the orange. Peel, then grate the carrots and put them in with the oranges. Tip in the cooled nuts and cumin seeds.

Whisk the captured orange juice with the oil, vinegar, poppy seeds (if using) and the honey, and toss this through the salad.

Prep time: 20 minutes
Cooking time: none
Serves: 4 as a side

SIZZLING STEAK SODA STACKS

The soda in the title refers to soda bread. You can choose a different type of bread, but make sure it's a fresh, crunchy-on-the-outside, soft-on-the-inside-bread, worthy of this king of hot steak sandwiches. The flavours covers all taste and texture bases, making it a barbecued sandwich to remember. Best of all, it's a doddle to make.

Ingredients

4 soda bread rolls

1 large red onion

2 tbsp balsamic vinegar

4 tbsp rapeseed or olive oil, plus extra for cooking

4 garlic cloves, skins on and crushed

1 large aubergine

2 heaped tsp smoked paprika

A good pinch of coarsely ground salt

4 minute steaks of a similar size to the bread rolls

2 large fresh tomatoes

4 tsp English mustard

Jar of gherkins (or make the cheat's version of pickled cucumber over the page)

Lettuce leaves

Method

Before the picnic Peel the onion and slice the top and roots off, being careful to not cut too much of the bottom off the onion. Now cut the onion into wedges, about 1cm thick. They should hold their shape if the bottom of the onion is still intact. Put them in a sealable freezer bag and add a tablespoon of oil, two tablespoons of balsamic vinegar and the crushed garlic cloves. Seal and put to one side.

Next, slice the aubergine into 1cm thick slices. Put these on a plate and pour a generous helping of oil over both sides, sprinkle with a little salt to flavour then rub in a couple of generous teaspoons of smoked paprika on both sides of the slices and put in a sealable tub.

At the picnic Wipe the grill with a little oil and heat it up. While it's heating, take two pieces of tin foil, each about the size of a magazine, place one on top of the other, and bend up at the edges to prevent liquid coming out. Put the onions and the liquid onto the centre of the foil.

Fold the foil over and seal the sides tightly to secure the parcel so that the liquid doesn't come out. You want a nice flat parcel with the onions spread out inside so that they all come into contact with the heat. ➤→

Prep time: 25 minutes
Cooking time: 10 minutes
Serves: 4

SIZZLING STEAK SODA STACKS

➤→ When the barbecue is hot, put the onion parcel and the pieces of aubergine on it to cook. If the barbecue has a lid, close it, as this will help things cook quicker.

After about 3 or 4 minutes, check that the onion isn't burning in the parcel by carefully prising open a corner. Turn the aubergine slices over. Both the onion and aubergine should be cooked and soft after about 8 to 10 minutes.

Take them off the griddle and cover to keep warm.

Keeping the grill hot, add the minute steaks and cook for about 30 seconds on each side, then check if they are cooked to your liking. If not, give them another 30 seconds on each side.

Cut the soda bread rolls in half, lay the open halves on the griddle to toast slightly.

Now construct your sandwich. First an aubergine slice, then the onions, then the steak spread with a little mustard, fresh tomato slices, some lettuce and gherkins and repeat with as much as you can get in.

Cheat's gherkin Slice half a cucumber, put the slices in a wide shallow bowl, cover with white wine vinegar, add a teaspoon of sugar and a few pinches of salt. Put in a sealable tub, leave for an hour then use as you would gherkin slices.

If you use a different cut of steak, increase the cooking time

MENU IDEAS

1

Mushroom burgers | Fiery nut and noodle salad | Banana and blueberry loaf cake

This griddle of goodies can be fully prepared at home. Pop the stuffed burgers on the grill and open the box of noodle salad – you can even re-heat the noodles in a foil dish.

2

Mediterranean lamb pasta | Chicken satay skewers | Mexican bean and pepper salad | Lemon and ginger cheesecake bites

Make this family feast before snuggling up under the stars in your tent. You can pop the bean salad in a foil dish on the grill if you prefer it hot.

3

Mackerel with rhubarb and salsa | Beetroot and celeriac slaw | New potato and broad bean salad | Orange zest brownies

For a beach barbecue, it's got to be fresh fish on the grill. Make all the extras in advance. Easy peasy.

4

Sizzling steak soda stacks | Marmalade chicken | Halloumi, watermelon and bulgur wheat salad | Orange and five spice coleslaw | Red, white and green pasta salad | Piña grillada | White peach sangria

Use this menu for a barbecue for a group. Nothing beats a gathering of happy, hungry friends around a grill.

MARVELLOUS PLACES

FOR THE

PERFECT
BARBECUE

—— BOLTON ABBEY ——

YORKSHIRE

The famous ruins of Bolton Abbey are an impressive backdrop for a barbecue. There is even a designated area to set up a grill at the southern end of the riverside car park, so you don't have to lug your kit too far from the car.

Steeped in some serious British history, it's a great place to explore after your food, with the atmospheric ruins of a 12th-century priory enveloped in myth, tragedy and legend. There's a wonderful riverside walk alongside the River Wharfe, as well as woodland and moorland. There is a majestic beauty about this whole landscape that captures the imagination, inspiring the artist JWM Turner and William Wordsworth, who wrote a poem about the place.

Designated bins provide safe disposal for barbecues when the ashes are cool. Picnic benches can be found in all estate car parks. There's a reasonable entrance fee for a carload (of up to 11 people), so it's worth the money to set up your barbecue and make a day of it.

FIND IT Bolton Abbey, Skipton, North Yorkshire, BD23 6EX. Bolton Abbey is just off the A59 between Skipton and Harrogate. The postcode brings you to Bolton Abbey village for access to Priory Church, ruins and walks to the riverside. Head for the southern end of the riverside car park for the barbecue area.

—— MERSEA ISLAND ——

ESSEX

It's hard to beat a beach barbecue at sunset. Cudmore Grove, on Mersea Island, has a secluded beach that allows barbecues. The sandy beach has impressive views across the mudflats with a host of wading birds, and is backed by a large open area of grassland for the children to run around and for the adults to relax. The area is rich in historic features, including World War II pillboxes and gun emplacements to hunt out.

FIND IT Bromans Lane, East Mersea, Essex, CO5 8UE.

—— YELLOWCRAIG BEACH ——

EAST LOTHIAN

Yellowcraig Beach (yes the sand is a yellow colour) is on the North Sea coast, east of Edinburgh, and is an unspoilt natural cove with views to the 1885 lighthouse on Fidra Island. The island was one of the inspirations for Robert Louis Stevenson's famous tale *Treasure Island*. This haven of coastline is popular with families as there's space to run around and rock pools to explore. Behind the beach is a play park and a network of footpaths through the sheltered woodlands, including a nature trail, and extensive grassland. There is a fire pit barbecue area near the beach that can be booked and paid for with the council. They will supply firewood (call 01620 827625 or email bookings@eastlothian.gov.uk).

FIND IT Dirleton, North Berwick, EH39 5DS. There is similar set up at John Muir country park, East Lothian, EH42 1X, where two barbecue stoves are available at Linkfield car park. Groups of 20 or more people should book in advance by calling 01368 866001.

—— CARDINHAM WOODS ——

BODMIN, CORNWALL

Brilliantly managed by the Forestry Commission, this 650-acre woodland is buzzing with wildlife: deer, buzzards, kingfishers and for the lucky few, otters have been spotted as well. It is the kind of place you discover and put on your list to come back to again and again, as it is so unspoilt and a fabulous breath of fresh air away from the stresses of everyday life. Cardinham Woods, just outside Bodmin, ticks all the boxes for a family day out with cycling and walking tracks, streams for dipping in and a play area with a free fire pit barbecue near the car parks for anyone to use.

FIND IT Nearest postcode is PL30 4AL. From Bodmin take the A38 towards Liskeard. 400 metres beyond the Carminnow Cross roundabout, follow the brown tourist signs left and then left again into Cardinham Woods. There's a large car park and toilet facilities at Cardinham, dogs are welcome.

—— RENDLESHAM FOREST ——

SUFFOLK

Rendlesham Forest is 1,500 hectares of mixed woodland, heath and wetland and a haven for nature enthusiasts, walkers and bird watchers alike. It is also more widely known as a spot where a series of reported sightings of unexplained lights in the sky became linked with fevered discussions of UFO landings in the 1980s. As a result, there is even an official UFO Trail for walkers to follow. There are family cycle tracks and a bike park too. Barbecues are welcome within the forest area car park and on the designated barbecue pads on the picnic benches. There is a metal bin for charcoal once it is cold. You can get a barbecue permit to fill in from the information hut in the car park when you get there.

FIND IT Rendlesham Forest, Woodbridge, Suffolk, IP12 3NF.

—— LYDIARD PARK ——

SWINDON

For a special occasion barbecue for a group of people, Lydiard Park is a winner. Admittedly you have to hire the static barbecue facilities (for half or whole days) but the surroundings are pretty special and the cost is reasonable if you need to guarantee a great spot for a large party.

Lydiard House has 260 acres of exquisite parkland, lakes, formal flower beds and green space on the western edge of Swindon. After eating, younger members of the party can make use of a great play area, or head off to explore the 18th-century house and walled gardens. There are often music events and outdoor theatre here, so it's a perfect location to make a full day of your barbecue picnic. Entry to the grounds of Lydiard Park is free, and dogs are welcome, although there is a fee for the house and the walled garden, and parking charges apply.

You can find the picnic and barbecue area to the right of the main car park off Hook Street. The barbecue season runs from 1st March to 31st October.

FIND IT Lydiard Park's postcode for directions is SN5 3PA. The park has two main entrances, Hay Lane and Hook Street. To book a barbecue call 01793 466664 or email lydiardpark@swindon.gov.uk.

NEW FOREST

HAMPSHIRE

A vast expanse of heath, ancient woodland, streams and rivers that stretches down to the sea, the New Forest is a collection of distinctly different zones to suit all activities. From grand tree-lined avenues and arboretums to quaint villages with free-roaming ponies, shaded glades with streams to open stretches of gorse-patched land for cricket games and group gathering. It has it all.

This ancient forest welcomes barbecuing in a selection of dedicated areas. There are also a couple of static barbecue sites that cater for up to 50 people, one at Anderwood and another at Wilverley, which you can book. Unsurprisingly the sites book up quickly in the summer, so two weeks notice is required to book either site.

You can use your own non-disposable barbecues on the gravel of any of the Forestry Commission car parks.

FIND IT Anderwood area postcode is BH24 4HS, Wilverley nearest postcode is BH24 4AZ. Email southern.permissions@forestry.gsi.gov.uk to book.

RAMSCOMBE

GREAT WOOD, RAMSCOMBE, SOMERSET

Encompassing soul-stirring landscapes of coastline, combe and coast, the Quantock Hills became England's first AONB (Area of Outstanding Natural Beauty) in 1956. It's a destination for lovers of the great outdoors, and in particular wildlife spotters, walkers and mountain bikers. As well as historic villages to explore and an interesting coastline, there are many forested landscapes with walking trails. One of these is the Great Wood, a large conifer and broadleaf wood with a two-mile 'red trail' through enormous Douglas Firs.

It's a popular spot for picnicking too. Head to Ramscombe car park at the heart of the woods; a short walk from here is a large open grassy space with a stream running alongside, providing plenty of entertainment for families. There are picnic tables and three barbecue pits provided.

FIND IT Access to Ramscombe for cars is via Adscombe Lane that starts between Marsh Mills and Over Stowey. It starts as a tarmac road (with a few sharp bends), then turns into a bit of a bumpy track once it enters the Quantocks – it all adds to the adventure. Nearest postcode is TA5 1HW.

—— SHELL ISLAND ——

GWYNEDD, NORTH WALES

Shell Island is on the north of Cardigan Bay, in Snowdonia National Park. Despite its name, it isn't actually an island as it can be reached by a causeway – except at high tide. Covering 450 acres, it was once a farm, but now 300 acres of it has been opened up as a campsite, albeit a wild one. People can pitch anywhere: fields, cliffs edges, dunes and next to the beach – it's a beautiful natural environment to find your own little piece of paradise. Day visitors are welcome and while there is still an entrance fee, it's worth it as you can have a campfire or barbecue on the beach, on the condition you clear up after yourselves. The bathing beaches are stunning, one of them backed by some of the tallest sand dunes in the country. A top beach barbecuing spot.

FIND IT Shell Island, Llanbedr, Gwynedd, LL45 2PJ.

—— MALLARDS PIKE ——

FOREST OF DEAN, GLOUCESTERSHIRE

Two man-made lakes are the central attraction at Mallards Pike. One of them is a boating lake. This pleasant area of the Forest of Dean has held the accolade of 'Best Picnic Spot in the UK' in a public survey held by Warburtons the bread makers. It is certainly a top spot that supports a good picnic, as there are picnic tables and a barbecuing area set next to the lake. After you've enjoyed a good grill, there are cycling and walking routes that take you around the lakes so you can burn off that lunch.

FIND IT The lake is near Blakeney on the A48, follow the signposts for Go Ape! (postcode GL15 4HD) once you pass Blakeney.

There are other designated barbecue areas in the Forest of Dean. Beechenhurst has three permanent gas barbecues for hire (tel 0300 067 4800). Wenchford has a barbecue site for your own barbecue (New Road, Blakeney). From the A48 at Blakeney take the B4431 Parkend Road. Three miles along this road you will find the site signposted on the right.

7
EXTRA PORTIONS

– DRESSINGS, – DIPS, SAUCES & SIDES

A homemade dressing can raise a bag of salad leaves to dizzy heights. Keep a collection of small glass jars with lids – they make the perfect dressing mixers and containers.

THAI LIME DRESSING

This is great with slices of barbecued steak served on a bed of leaves, strips of cucumber and spring onion, and a scattering of chopped red chilli.

Ingredients

4 tbsp fresh lime juice

2 tbsp soy sauce

2 tbsp fish sauce

2 tbsp sesame oil

2 tbsp freshly chopped coriander

2 tbsp freshly chopped mint

½ small red chilli, very finely chopped

Method

Put all the ingredients in a jam jar and shake vigorously. As you are using fresh herbs, this dressing needs to be used the day you make it. Or add the herbs just before serving.

HONEY, MUSTARD & THYME DRESSING

This is lovely over cooled green beans or in a grated carrot salad.

Ingredients

3 tbsp wholegrain mustard

¼ garlic glove, grated

4 tbsp good olive oil

2 tbsp runny honey

A sprig of fresh thyme, leaves only

Method

Put all of the ingredients into a jam jar and shake vigorously, ensuring that all the honey has mixed in.

MUSTARD VINAIGRETTE

Perfect for a chicken salad.

Ingredients

½ garlic clove, minced

½ tsp salt flakes

2 tsp Dijon mustard

5 tbsp olive oil

2 tbsp red wine vinegar

Method

On a chopping board, mix the salt with the minced garlic clove using a butter knife so that you achieve a garlic purée. Put this in a jam jar with the mustard, olive oil and red wine vinegar and shake it vigorously. Make sure it is fully combined.

SPICY SALAD DRESSING

Great for lentil and roasted pepper salads. Mix a tray of roasted red onion, red and yellow peppers with a jar of drained puy lentils. Mix through this dressing and crumble feta across the top.

Ingredients

2 tbsp lemon juice

5 tbsp olive oil

½ tsp harissa paste (or more if you want it hotter)

Salt and black pepper

Method

Put in a jam jar and shake to combine.

BEETROOT & MINT DIP

Pink, pretty and rather tasty.

Serves 2

Ingredients

80g cooked beetroot, not the soaked in vinegar sort

60g full fat cream cheese

Zest of ½ unwaxed lemon

4 mint leaves, with a couple to garnish

½ garlic clove

Large pinch of sea salt and black pepper

Method

Put all the ingredients into a hand mixer, blend until smooth and decant into a little tub with a lid. Decorate with the extra mint leaves.

ROASTED RED PEPPER & WALNUT DIP

A scarlet-red dip to add to your picnic spread. If you want to liven things up, add a quarter of a teaspoon of finely chopped fresh red chilli or a pinch or two of dried chilli flakes.

Serves 2

Ingredients

150g red peppers

½ tsp smoked sweet paprika

1 tsp soft brown sugar

1 tsp balsamic vinegar

50g walnut halves

Large pinch of sea salt

Coarsely ground black pepper

Method

Take the stalks off the peppers and deseed them. Cut into quarters lengthways. Generously drizzle with oil and use your hands to rub the oil all over the peppers and put in a roasting tin. Add a little salt and pepper and roast in the pre-heated oven at 200°C/Fan 180°C/400°F/Gas mark 6 for 25 to 30 minutes until softened, turning occasionally. Take out and allow to cool.

Many people prefer to peel the skins off the peppers at this stage. I like to leave them on as I think they add flavour and texture.

Combine all ingredients together using a hand blender or food processor to blend until smooth. If needed, add more salt and pepper to taste.

BEETROOT & CELERIAC SLAW

Ingredients

3 medium beetroot, peeled and grated

1 celeriac, peeled and grated

4 tbsp half fat crème fraîche

2 tbsp horseradish cream (shop-bought or see right for recipe)

2 tbsp lemon juice

Method

Put the grated celeriac and grated beetroot into a bowl. Mix the crème fraîche, the horseradish cream and lemon juice together then add it to the bowl of celeriac and beetroot. Transfer this to a tub with a lid.

HOMEMADE TARTARE SAUCE

Serve with the gin-baked salmon on page 90

Ingredients

6 tbsp baby cornichons, sliced

6 tbsp capers

1 tsp unwaxed lemon zest

2 tbsp fresh dill, chopped

600ml crème fraîche

2 garlic cloves, roasted with skins on alongside the salmon

Method

Mix the sliced cornichons, capers, dill and lemon zest with the crème fraîche. Squeeze the cooked garlic out of their skins, then chop and mash up the garlic flesh to mix into the sauce as well.

HORSERADISH CREAM

Serve with the scarlet salmon on page 180

Ingredients

100ml double cream

1 tsp horseradish sauce

1 tsp finely grated white or red onion (messy, but worth it for the flavour)

½ tsp Dijon mustard

½ tsp caster sugar

1 tbsp white wine vinegar

2 tsp finely chopped tarragon

Pinch of salt

Method

Whip the double cream into soft peaks then stir all the other ingredients into the cream. Decant into a lidded tub and chill until you need it.

– PASTRY –

SWEET SHORTCRUST PASTRY

Makes enough for eight strawberry tarts on page 64

Ingredients

200g plain flour

125g chilled butter, cut into small cubes

40g icing sugar

1 large egg yolk

Method

Sift the flour and icing sugar together and mix this with the cold butter in an electric mixer. When it starts to resemble breadcrumbs, add the egg yolk and mix until it starts to come together. Turn off the mixer and use your hands to gather up all the mixture and form it into a ball of dough. Wrap in cling film and put in the fridge for 30 minutes until you are ready to use it.

SHORTCRUST PASTRY 1

Makes enough for six salmon and asparagus tartlets on page 58

Ingredients

210g plain flour

½ tsp salt

50g chilled butter, cut into small cubes

50g chilled lard, cut into small cubes

Chilled water

1 tbsp double cream (optional)

Method

Sift the flour and salt into a bowl. Add the cubes of lard and butter. Use an electric mixer on the slow setting to mix it together until it looks like large breadcrumbs. Or you can use your fingers to rub it all in.

Add one tablespoon of very cold water and a tablespoon of double cream (if you want a rich pastry) and bring it together with your hands. If it is still too crumbly, add more water, a tablespoon at a time until it binds together. Form it into a ball, wrap in cling film and put in the fridge to chill for 30 minutes.

SHORTCRUST PASTRY 2

Makes enough for Mum's picnic pie on page 102

Ingredients

340g plain flour

1 level tsp salt

85g chilled butter, cut into small cubes

85g chilled lard, cut into small cubes

Chilled water

1 egg yolk

Method

Sift the flour and salt into a large bowl, then rub the cubes of butter and lard into the flour using your fingertips until it looks like breadcrumbs.

Beat the egg yolk and add this to the mixture, adding a couple of tablespoons of cold water to help it all bind together. Use your hands to bring it together to make a ball. Wrap it in cling film and put it in the fridge for 15 minutes.

– DRINKS –

Some easy-to-prepare drinks for your picnic. Some boozy, some not.

All drinks serve 4

SIMPLE ELDERFLOWER CORDIAL RECIPE

This lovely seasonal cordial can be mixed with sparkling water or wine for a summery drink to go with your picnic or barbecue. This makes a 1.5 litre bottle of cordial.

Ingredients

2kg caster sugar

About 30 elderflower heads

2 unwaxed lemons, chopped into large chunks

1 unwaxed orange, chopped into large chunks

90g citric or tartaric acid (available from chemists)

Method

Put the sugar in a very large mixing bowl or preserving pan and pour 1.5 litres of boiling water over it. Stir well to dissolve the sugar and set aside to cool.

Add the flowerheads, lemons, oranges and citric acid. Mix gently.

Leave in a cool place to infuse for 24 hours.

Strain the liquid through some muslin and transfer to sterilised bottles, seal tightly and keep chilled.

Dilute with still or sparkling water or sparkling wine.

ELDERFLOWER COLLINS

This is inspired by those mid-summer camping trips when the hedgerows hang heavy with fragrant elderflowers. Most farm shops sell lovely versions of elderflower cordials that can be used to make this delicious cocktail, or make your own version from the previous recipe.

Ingredients

240ml gin

80ml lemon juice

60ml elderflower cordial

Sugar syrup – see below

Soda water or tonic to top up

Lemon slices and fresh mint to serve

Method

For the sugar syrup, put eight tablespoons of caster sugar and eight tablespoons of water together in a pan and heat, stirring until all the sugar is dissolved. Cool before using.

Vigorously mix (or shake) the gin, lemon juice, cordial and syrup together and refrigerate.

When serving, pour into a tall glass, top up with tonic and garnish with a slice of lemon and sprig of mint.

MANGO BELLINIS

Perfect for a picnic at an open-air concert. Definitely one for the posh hamper.

Ingredients

1 ripe mango

1 bottle of Prosecco

Method

Peel and chop one large, ripe mango and put it in a blender with 200ml of Prosecco. You should end up with a fruit purée. Pour this into a transportable container or bottle.

At the picnic, divide the purée between four cocktail glasses then top up with Prosecco.

PALE PEACH SANGRIA

A lighter, white wine version of sangria that feels right for sunny picnics.

Ingredients

750ml chilled white wine (something aromatic like a Riesling is good)

125ml peach schnapps

4 tbsp brandy

500ml chilled ginger ale

3 tbsp caster sugar

2 ripe peaches, cut into slices

2 oranges, cut into slices

1 lime, cut into slices

A sprig of fresh mint leaves

Method

You will need a large jug to make and serve this in, plus bottles to transport it in your cool box. I put mine in tea flasks!

Add the peach schnapps and brandy to the wine and stir in the sugar. Add the fruit and put it in the fridge to cool for at least an hour before leaving for your picnic. Put the ginger ale in the fridge to cool too.

Combine the ale with the wine in a pitcher at the picnic and garnish with fresh mint leaves

COCONUT, CUCUMBER, GINGER & LIME COOLER

For the hottest of days, this is a brilliant drink to refresh, revive and rehydrate your picnic party.

Ingredients

1 litre coconut water

8 tbsp lime juice

2 cucumbers, sliced thinly

1 tbsp fresh ginger, finely grated

100g caster sugar

A handful of chopped fresh mint leaves

Method

Combine all of the ingredients, apart from the mint leaves, in a large jug and put in the fridge to cool for at least an hour before decanting to flasks to take to your picnic. Mix the mint leaves into the drink just before serving.

INDEX

PICNIC SPOTS

—ACKNOWLEDGEMENTS—

A hearty thank you to my family, Gavin, Maisy and Mack for eating picnic food for breakfast, lunch and tea for months, but mostly for your smiles, patience and humour to keep me on track during long hours at stove and screen. Long live kitchen discos.

James Tims, we are still laughing. It's a good sign. Thank you for the photography, the patience, the enthusiasm and the hours. Clare Ashton, my editor, thank you for your calming guidance through my creative chaos.

I am so gratefully indebted to a loyal army of recipe makers, testers and tasters. My mum, Christine Shire, James' mum, Christine Tims, Tanya Tims (thanks for letting us invade your home on a regular basis), Sophia Tims, Nicole Pike, Emma Pike, Sarah Adey-Peters, Helen Jenkins, Liz Haynes, Rebecca Needes, Jade Pickard, Daisy Triner, the Pate family and all who helped – thank you very much.

Luckily, everyone seems to have a happy picnic story. As a result, I have had the most fantastic response from friends and family keen to share their top spots and picnic tips. Thank you all, a sausage roll is in the post. In particular, to my wonderful and well-travelled parents-in-law Frank and Trish Unsworth, Gemma Evans, Simon McGrath, Rebecca Nunn, James Irwin, Sally Manning, Helen Wooldridge, Sally Peaches, Tim Livesey, Ben Turner, Dee Robinson, Carl Arrowsmith and Victoria Cole.

A hamper full of love and gratitude goes to Mum and Tad for taking me and my brother Mike on many picnics to the New Forest when we were little, and for all the very happy memories those created. It's where the picnic love started.

And, on behalf of us all, a thank you to all the people who work in the woodlands at the Forestry Commission for enabling us to have access to so many magical spots to lay down our rugs. We are very grateful. You do an amazing job.

Finally, thanks be to gin.